The author with John Duke

AMERICAN ART SONG
and
AMERICAN POETRY

Volume II:
Voices of Maturity

Ruth C. Friedberg

The Scarecrow Press, Inc.
Metuchen, N.J., & London
1984

ACKNOWLEDGMENTS

From The Poetry of Robert Frost edited by Edward Connery Lathem. Copyright 1928, 1934, © 1969 by Holt, Rinehart and Winston. Copyright © 1956, 1962 by Robert Frost. Reprinted by permission of Holt, Rinehart and Winston, Publishers. Also to the Estate of Robert Frost, Jonathan Cape Ltd. From The Complete Poems of Emily Dickinson, edited by Thomas H. Johnson. Copyright 1929 by Martha Dickinson Bianchi; Copyright © renewed 1957 by Mary L. Hampson. Reprinted by permission of Little, Brown and Company. Musical examples 3.5, 3.6, 3.7, 3.8, 3.9, 3.10, 3.37, 3.38, 3.39, 3.40, 3.41, 3.42, 3.43, 3.44, 3.45, 3.46, used by permission of the Southern Music Publishing Co. Inc., are separately acknowledged below each example. Added to each of these is the following: International Copyright Secured. All Rights Reserved Including the Right of Public Performance. Musical examples 4.41, 4.42, 4.43, 4.44, 4.45, 4.46, used by permission of European American Music Distributors Corporation, are separately acknowledge below each example. Added to each of these is the following: Copyright renewed 1965 by Paul Nordoff. All rights reserved. EAMDC is the sole U.S. agent for Schott & Co. Ltd., London.

Library of Congress Cataloging in Publication Data
(Revised for volume 2)

Friedberg, Ruth C., 1928–
    American art song and American poetry.

    Includes bibliographies and indexes.
    Contents: v. 1. America comes of age -- v. 2. Voices of maturity.
    1. Songs--United States--History and criticism.
I. Title.
ML2811.F75   784.3'00973   81-9047
ISBN 0-8108-1460-9 (v. 1)
ISBN 0-8108-1682-2 (v. 2)

To S. J. F.

CONTENTS

FOREWORD

Volume I of this series pinpointed America's "coming of age" in the art song by a process of integrating indigenous American elements with those of our European heritage. This musical declaration of independence having been delineated, Volume II will treat, from a chronological perspective, composers born just before or after the turn of the century, who begin in the 1920's and continue for the next several decades to respond to the flood of American poetry becoming available to them. Mary Howe, although somewhat older than the rest of this group, merits inclusion historically, since she did not undertake serious composition until the age of forty, and was therefore writing during the same period.

The author's focus, as stated in Volume I, continues to be "the interrelationships between the composer and the poet and the ways in which these have influenced the completed song" in selected examples which "are not only important contributions to the performing literature, but also illuminate some phase of America's cultural past." Once again, there has been considerable effort expended on personal interview and correspondence, which has resulted in the presentation of much previously unpublished material. Discussions, therefore, of composers' lives, their journalistic publications, and their connections to the poets (as well as the complex social and professional links within the worlds of poetry and of musical composition) will be more extensively developed than in Volume I. Where settings are included of a poet who has already had a major discussion in this volume or the previous one, reference is given and the material is not repeated. New facts or interpretations concerning this poet may, however, be brought in when pertinent to the new composer and setting.

Discerning readers may observe that several promised Volume II composers have been omitted, but let them be reassured that these figures have not been forgotten, merely delayed until Volume III. The reason for this is the emergence, during the writing, of the necessity for a two-chapter treatment of John Duke, whose career, articulate statements concerning art song, and important settings of large numbers of American poets, have not heretofore been adequately presented.

Paul Bowles, David Diamond, Samuel Barber, and Vincent Persichetti will appear, then, in the third volume, along with Ned Rorem, William Flanagan, Thomas Pasatieri, and John Corigliano, Jr., as previously projected. Several others of the more recent composers will be added to this group, and the listing of Volume III poets will include (but not be limited to) Herman Melville, James Agee, Tennessee Williams, Stephen Crane, Wallace Stevens, and Edward Albee.

It will be apparent from the Notes that a number of the songs under consideration (particularly those published before 1950) are already out of print. Where this occurs, I have indicated library collections or other sources whenever they are available. I should like to emphasize that this is all extremely important literature from both the performing and historical points of view, and that it must not be lost when it has scarcely been found.

My thanks to Professor Gerard Jaffe for his ongoing suggestions, and to Pat Cooper for her assistance in the preparation of this manuscript.

Ruth C. Friedberg

AMERICAN ART SONG AND AMERICAN POETRY

Volume II: Voices of Maturity

Virgil Thomson, the author, and John Igo, October 4, 1981, during an interview prior to a performance of The Mother of Us All at Incarnate Word College, San Antonio, Texas

INTRODUCTION

Two major events of the twentieth century's second decade were to have a profound effect on American song composers. One was World War I, and the other, the beginning of the American poetic renaissance. War in Europe meant that the obligatory pilgrimage to German conservatories was no longer possible, and once the pattern had been broken, it was never reinstated. In actuality, the necessity for foreign training no longer existed, for American conservatories and university departments of music, often staffed by European born and/or trained faculty, were growing in numbers, size, and quality.

In these pages, then, we will find that Mary Howe and John Duke chose, from their mid-Atlantic origins, to study at the Peabody Conservatory; Ross Lee Finney stayed in Minnesota for undergraduate training at the state University and Carleton College; Virgil Thomson came east to Harvard from St. Louis; while Charles Naginski, Sergius Kagen, and Paul Nordoff congregated at the newly established Juilliard School in New York City. It is, of course, likewise true that a number of American composers, including Thomson, Duke, and Finney, took their newly acquired technical competence to Paris for periods of study with Nadia Boulanger, who not only passed on to them the twentieth-century French traditions (including Stravinsky's neo-classicism) but also encouraged their own experimentation in the search for the unique creative self. None, however, with the exception of Virgil Thomson, stayed in Paris, and there emerged no colony of American musical expatriates to parallel the "lost" literary generation.

One very plausible explanation for this may be that

3

despite the many economic upheavals of the period, there was considerable musical excitement to be found at home. The twenties and thirties saw not only the rise of the conservatories and university departments, but also a centering of musical energy around summer activities at the MacDowell, Yaddo, and Seagle colonies and the festivals which they generated. Aaron Copland and Roger Sessions carried their championship of American music into a series of New York concerts, and Sessions became the mentor of a number of younger composers seeking to extend their grasp of avant-garde technique.

Beside and beyond all this, and of prime importance to the song composer, was the flood of poetry which began to pour from American writers in the early twentieth century. This phenomenon, since termed the American poetic renaissance,[1] was certainly equal in size and quality to the products of German Romanticism and the French Symbolists. In similar fashion, it provided the inspiration for the large body of American art song which followed, and which, in fact, is still being written today.

Much of the vitality of this poetic movement will be seen to originate from the attempt to infuse new forms and philosophies into the calcified traditions of the Victorians. E. A. Robinson makes a beginning with his dramatic, regional portraits of New Englanders, and this is extended by Robert Frost whose "plain speech" is still contained within familiar poetic structures. Sandburg goes still further and adapts Whitman's free verse to the harsh, urban world of the twentieth century, while Amy Lowell and Marianne Moore flirt with the Imagist emphasis on objective reality.

Another spring feeding into this poetic river is the major contribution made by women writers who find poetry an important medium for expression of the early impulses toward "liberation." With E. R. A. and even women's suffrage in the historical future, Sara Teasdale struggles to integrate her artistic life with her perceptions of the female role in society, while Adelaide Crapsey easily wins academic and literary stature, only to fall prey to her own mortality. Edna St. Vincent Millay and Elinor Wylie break free of convention but find that freedom carries burdens, as it does to their male counterparts; Millay's poetry records the painful knowledge, and Wylie's, her attempt to master it.

A major force which emerges in support of this burst

4

of poetic activity proves to be the "little magazines," those periodicals aimed at a small group of discriminating readers whose ancestor was The Dial of 1840-1844, edited by Ralph Waldo Emerson and Margaret Fuller. It is undoubtedly true that "writers were never before received and encouraged to continue as they have been in the little magazines of our century."[2] This volume will refer many times over to Harriet Monroe's Chicago-based Poetry, founded in 1912, which fought for Imagism and free verse in its early days, and presented some of the first published work of Frost, Sandburg, Moore, Millay, and Wylie. Reedy's Mirror of St. Louis will appear in connection with publications of Teasdale and Millay, and The Egoist of London with Imagist writers of the 'teens.

Almost inseparable from American artistic history of the twenties is The Dial, reconstituted in 1921 by Scott Thayer and Sibley Watson, and destined to prominence as the birthplace of the "new" literary criticism, as a source of encouragement for the experimental in all forms of art, and as the yearly purveyor of The Dial award for significant literary contribution. Many connections to The Dial will be forthcoming among the writers and composers of this volume, for Marianne Moore was its editor from 1925 to 1929, e.e. cummings and Conrad Aiken frequent contributors of poetry and reviews, and Virgil Thomson a sought-after but unwilling addition to its staff of writers.

Surrounded, therefore, by this vast treasure-house of recent lyric poetry as well as the newly discovered legacies of Whitman and Dickinson from the last century, the American composers could not help responding with their own explosion into song. Many catalogs become swollen with settings of English-language and primarily American poetry: John Duke, at 84, has recently completed #252. Except for a dedicated group of "Americanists,"[3] the majority of these composers have not attempted a consciously ethnic style based on specific quotations from the hymns, ballads, or popular literatures. They work, instead, to integrate the newer twentieth-century elements of flexible meter (the musical counterpart of free verse), Impressionism, neo-classicism, late Romantic chromaticism, and its serial derivatives into a language that will adapt to the prosodic and expressive needs of the poetic texts. The staggering variety of their success will be evident in what follows, as America's voice, in maturity, is seen to absorb the parochial, and, like all the highest forms of artistic expression, approach the universal.

5

NOTES

1. For a detailed discussion of the "poetic renaissance," its forerunners, and descendants, see: Horace Gregory and Marya Zaturenska, A History of American Poetry: 1900-1940 (New York: Harcourt, Brace, 1942).

2. Hoffman, Allen, and Ulrich, The Little Magazine (Princeton, New Jersey: Princeton University Press, 1947), p. 229.

3. See Volume I of this series, Chapters III and IV, for a discussion of Charles Ives and the "Americanists" who derived from his work.

I. TWO AMERICAN ORIGINALS

Mary Howe and Virgil Thomson were both born in the waning decades of the nineteenth century. Despite this fact they did not "sum up" the creative achievements of the preceding age but, on the contrary, were both in the vanguard of new waves that, in the twentieth century, were to flood the American musical scene with fresh life.

One of Howe's principal biographers, Madeleine Goss, states that "chronologically Mary Howe belongs to the earlier group of American composers; but her work actually places her in a later period, for it is definitely modern in style."[1] This is especially evident in Howe's songs, in which her fresh harmonic language and rhythmic treatments combine with a discriminating ear for the finest poetry of the new American lyricists. Her status as an "original" must also be partly attributed to the fact that, while leading a rich family life, she managed to cultivate her own creative gifts with energy and devotion many years before the emergence of the historical phenomenon known as the "woman's liberation movement."

Virgil Thomson, another unique figure, embodies the surprising evolution of the son of a Kansas City post office clerk into a focal member of the most sophisticated Parisian artistic circles of the twenties and thirties. Eventually he was also to become an arbiter of musical taste in the United States, at the same time revolutionizing American vocal music with a totally new approach to the setting of English language texts.

Howe and Thomson had each studied for a time in Paris with Nadia Boulanger, the gifted nurturer of compositional originality, yet their musical styles were light years apart. The poets that drew them are equally different, and the settings that resulted are a part of the magnificent diversity that is American song in its Voices of Maturity.

Mary Howe (1882-1964)
Elinor Wylie (1885-1928), Amy Lowell (1874-1925)

Mary Howe was a resident of Washington, D.C. throughout her life, although she had been born in her maternal grandmother's house in Richmond, Virginia. Her father, Calderon Carlisle, was an international lawyer of Scottish descent, her mother's ancestry was Welsh, and a touch of Spanish blood entered the family through the marriage of a great-aunt on the paternal side. Like many well-bred young women of her time, Mary Howe was educated totally at home, and one of her most important early influences was a Frenchwoman named Mlle. Seron who was her music instructor.[2]

As a girl she made frequent trips to Europe, and during one of these she studied the piano in Dresden with Richard Burmeister. Somewhat later she worked with Ernest Hutcheson and Harold Randolph at the Peabody Institute in Baltimore. In 1912 she married Walter Bruce Howe, a Washington lawyer like her father, who "knew very little about music but was totally supportive of his wife's musical activities."[3] Interestingly, it was three years after her marriage that she made her professional debut playing as half of a two-piano team. The other member of the duo was Anne Hull, who at this writing is 94 years old and lives in Westport, Conn. The two women soloed with several leading orchestras, including the Cleveland, Baltimore, and National Symphonies, and when Mary Howe began to compose, music for two pianos was to be one of her favorite genres.

Madeleine Goss gives a detailed and absorbing account of the years during which Howe juggled the care of home and three young children with work toward her diploma in composition under Peabody's Gustav Strube.[4] Since her early education had been entirely at home, the final examination which she took for this diploma was the first she had ever experienced.[5] She passed this hurdle in 1922 and found herself, at the age of forty, beginning the productive part of her life as a creative artist.

During the next three decades Mary Howe composed an impressive catalog of vocal works, both solo and choral, and instrumental works for solo piano, two pianos, various chamber groups, and orchestra.[6] Her first public notice occurred at the Worcester Music Festival in 1925 with the performance of "Chain Gang Song." This was a choral piece inspired by the sight of a group of black prisoners that Howe had encountered many years earlier while riding horseback in the North Carolina mountains. Her reputation continued to grow through the performance of many of her orchestral compositions by symphonies of the stature of the New York Philharmonic, Chicago, Philadelphia, and BBC. Dr. Hans Kindler of the National Symphony, who was especially interested in programming contemporary American composers, premièred a number of Howe's works.

All the while, her catalog of songs was growing steadily. Mary Howe was a voracious reader and owned many volumes of poetry.[7] Her affinity to words included German and French poetry as well as English, as is demonstrated by the contents of her major publication of forty-nine songs in seven volumes:[8]

Volume I	Seven Goethe Songs (German)
Volume II	English Songs: Part One
Volume III	Baritone Songs (English)
Volume IV	French Songs
Volume V	German Songs
Volume VI	English Songs: Part Two
Volume VII	English Songs: Part Three

Each of these seven volumes contains seven songs, and the poetic choices range through four centuries. Shakespeare, Goethe, Tennyson, Victor Hugo, Baudelaire, and Rilke are among those represented, as well as Mary Howe herself in one setting, and Wylie and Lowell in six of the songs we shall examine.

Howe and Elinor Wylie were born only three years apart, and the poet's family had moved to Washington, D. C. from Philadelphia when she was twelve. Mary Howe knew her during these years of their girlhood and in later years, as a connoisseur of poetry, was attracted by the quality of Wylie's work and by its adaptability to musical setting. The MacDowell colony was another likely connection between Mary Howe, Elinor Wylie, and Amy Lowell as well. Howe, as an active musical philanthropist, was on the board of directors of the MacDowell Association and did much of her composing at the Colony in the summertime. Elinor Wylie also spent several summers there writing both prose and poetry in the seclusion which the Colony offered. Both Wylie and Lowell gave readings of their poetry at the MacDowell Club in New York to benefit the Colony[9] and it is not unlikely that the three women crossed paths in the course of their activities supporting this enterprise.

Elinor Wylie's background was very similar to Mary Howe's. She had distinguished Philadelphia ancestry on both sides of the family, and her father, Henry Martyn Hoyt, was to become solicitor general of the United States. When Elinor was two years old, the Hoyts moved to Rosemont, an affluent "Main Line" suburb of Philadelphia, and enrolled her in private school in Bryn Mawr. This type of education continued during her Washington years, and when she was eighteen, her grandfather took her and her sister Constance for a season in Paris and London.

Here the similarity to Mary Howe ends. In direct contrast to the composer's long, stable marriage, Elinor Wylie's personal life was stormy and highly unconventional for her time, causing her to live for many years as an outcast from the social milieu into which she had been born. At the age of twenty she had been prodded into marrying Philip Hichborn, a wealthy young Washingtonian who proved to be mentally unstable. They had one son who was to be reared by Hichborn's family, for in 1910 the poet eloped with Horace Wylie who was married and fifteen years her senior. The couple lived in England in virtual isolation under an assumed name until 1915. During this time, Horace Wylie opened the world of literature, history, and philosophy to Elinor, and created a life in which she could have been relatively happy had it not been for the snubs of English "society,"[10] Horace's ambivalence about his wife and children,[11] and the disquieting news, in 1912, of Hichborn's suicide.

World War I forced the couple to return to America, where Horace's wife finally agreed to a divorce and enabled them to marry. Still unacceptable to her former circle in Washington, Elinor Wylie gradually became a darling of the New York literary scene, as her writing, her beauty, and her dramatic personality began to be known. In 1921 she divorced Horace Wylie, and in 1923 married the poet William Rose Benét, who was a widower with three children. They had a few years of domestic life in Connecticut and New York City during which her restlessness and severe headaches, caused by chronic high blood pressure, continued unabated. After this she was drawn increasingly back to England and to a new romantic relationship which was cut short by her untimely death from the third of a series of strokes.

Mary Colum describes the moving occasion of the private funeral in William Rose Benét's apartment, with Elinor Wylie laid out in a favorite silver dress that still provided striking contrast to her flaming red hair. Present were not only the mother who had never entirely approved of her famous daughter and the son whom she had rarely seen since his infancy, but also such other creative artists of her circle as Douglas Moore and Edna St. Vincent Millay.[12] It was an appropriately dramatic farewell for this woman whose turbulent life had made inroads on her health and nervous stability but had left intact her remarkable courage, intellect, and artistry.

All of Elinor Wylie's major poetry (four volumes) was produced during the final eight years of her life. A book entitled Collected Poems, published in 1931, contained this work plus a group of "Hitherto Uncollected Poems" and an introductory memoir by William Rose Benét. The decade that followed saw a steady stream of Mary Howe's settings of these poems, two of which were written for chorus in 1936: "Spring Pastoral" for women's voices with piano (later transcribed for orchestra) and "Robin Hood's Heart" for men's voices with piano.[13]

The three Wylie settings for solo voice from the middle thirties--"Little Elegy" (1934), "Let Us Walk in the White Snow" (1935), and "When I Died in Berners Street" (1936)[14]-- are among Mary Howe's finest works and demonstrate that unmistakable affinity of composer for poet which is all too rarely encountered in the song medium. All three of these poems show the typical Wylie preference for short lines and compact verse forms which served to "compress and intensify expression."[15] In the opinion of this writer, it is this very compression which has made Elinor Wylie's poetry (like Emily Dickinson's) so appropriate for musical setting, since the verbal tautness allows and invites musical amplification by the composer.

"Little Elegy" comes from Wylie's last volume of verse, Angels and Earthly Creatures, which was published posthumously in 1929. It was from this collection that the poet, newly returned to America, read to a group of close friends two nights before her death, confiding to Mary Colum that a developing relationship with a man in England had inspired many of the poems. "Little Elegy," an extremely concise yet moving tribute to this relationship, contains only ten lines of very regular iambic dimeter. In the opening lines

> "Withouten you
> No rose can grow"

Wylie chooses to use the Middle English form of "without" which serves a double purpose of filling out the poetic foot while it establishes an atmosphere of ancient and universal meaning.

The fact that Mary Howe made alternate settings of this text with piano and with string quartet[16] suggests its basically linear conception and the close interweaving of vocal and instrumental lines. Howe's lyrical gift and sensitivity to the poetic phrase is demonstrated by the individual contour of these lines. Form is imposed on this lyricism partially through a four note opening phrase ("Withouten you") announced by voice and piano.

Example 1.1, measures 1-5. Copyright © 1939, G. Schirmer, Inc.; used by permission.

This phrase recurs several times throughout the song (once in inversion) and has its last statement in augmentation in the piano part, serving to emphasize the final word, "nowhere" (see Example 1.2).

In examining rhythmic aspects of this song, we find that Mary Howe's setting has completely swallowed or "assimilated"[17] the original poetic form. The iambic dimeter has disappeared by virtue of the longer note values assigned to words at the end of each poetic line (see Example 1.1). Even the overall structure of the ten line verse form has disappeared because of musical repetitions such as the following:

Example 1.2, measures 21-28. Copyright © 1939, G. Schirmer, Inc.; used by permission.

However, the aesthetic result of these changes, as in all successful settings, is not a sense of loss, but rather one of "synthesis," to use Donald Ivey's term.[18] One senses that the condensed emotion of the poem has been musically released and amplified, much in the manner of Robert Schumann's handling of the similarly terse Heine texts.

Finally, two harmonic devices serve to further strengthen this setting. The first is the composer's use of chordal appogiaturas just before the pianistic interludes to build tension behind climactic words such as "sing."

Example 1.3, measures 15-17. Copyright © 1939, G. Schirmer, Inc.; used by permission.

The second is the surprising enharmonic change from G-sharp to A-flat that occurs on the first "nowhere," marked misterioso to underline the strangeness of the sound and the poetic idea. In repetition, "nowhere" is set with a lowered second degree, whose nearness to the tonic suggests the meagreness of life without the subject of the "elegy" (see Example 1.2).

"Let Us Walk in the White Snow" is the first line of "Velvet Shoes," perhaps Elinor Wylie's best-known poem, and is also the title which Mary Howe assigned to her setting of it, written in 1935. Here again, Howe composed accompaniments for piano or string quartet[19] and indeed, much of the keyboard writing is in a spare, four part, non-pianistic style which could well relate to a prospective string adaptation. "Velvet Shoes" contains slightly longer lines than "Little Elegy" and there are four stanzas of five lines each which Mary Howe sets word for word without omissions, additions, or repetitions.

In this, Wylie's "virtuoso piece," the "relatively unob-

14

trusive ... prosodic effects" are indeed impressive as she slows down her basic, quickly moving, anapestic meter with extra unaccented and heavily accented syllables.[20] Mary Howe achieves this same plastic flow in musical terms by employing a flexible 5/8 rhythm that frequently alternates with 2/8, 4/8, etc. This allows for an extremely wide range of possibilities in shortening and lengthening syllables based on eighth-note increments.

Example 1.4, measures 1-9. Copyright 1948, Carl Fischer, Inc.; used by permission.

This type of rhythmic organization is interrupted only by the setting of

"Silence will fall like dews
On white silence below."

Here the composer applies musical word-painting to the concept of "silence" by achieving a falling off of sound both pitch-wise, through the descent of an octave, and dynamically through the decrescendo. Note that the effect is reinforced by its repetition with the second appearance of the word "si-

15

Example 1.5, measures 59-66. Copyright 1948, Carl Fischer, Inc.; used by permission.

lence." It is also intensified by the longer note lengths of this passage which trail off to nothing, and by the diminished participation of the piano.

Harmonic imagery also plays an important part in Howe's setting of this poem. Appropriately, she chooses the "whitest" of keys, C major, but with the opening measures she has already begun to add the diatonic and eventually chromatic nonchord tones which prevail throughout the song (see Example 1.4). Interestingly, the aural effect of this harmonic cloudiness seems not to endanger the "whiteness" of the setting, but rather to add a softness analogous to the textures of "velvet," "silk," and "wool" and a wandering quality which suggests the aimlessness of snow-impeded walking.

The third of these three poems displays still another aspect of Wylie's writing to place alongside the constricted emotional fervor of "Little Elegy" and the virtuosic, word-

16

intoxicated tribute to austerity of sensation that is "Velvet Shoes." The occasional obscurity of meaning in her poetry, despite the unfailing clarity of her language, is attributed by Mary Colum to the fact that Elinor Wylie always wrote out of highly complex thought processes.[21] "When I Died in Berners Street" is the setting of such a poem, and its original poetic title of "A Strange Story" gives one the clue that some effort will have to be applied by the reader in order to penetrate its strangeness. The poem has six stanzas, which Howe sets unchanged, except for the omission of the word "but" at the beginning of verses two and five. Each of the stanzas describes an imagined death in one of six different places. The missing piece of the puzzle is that all these places are various sections of London, a city that the poet knew well, both from the years of her exile with Horace Wylie, and from her frequent trips to England during the final years of her life.

The poem is a masterful portrait, again with unobtrusive but skillful metric control, of not one character, but six, whose lives are swiftly and colorfully evoked by the scenes of their passing. In one of the most dramatic settings of the twentieth century, Mary Howe selects a straightforward 4/4 meter and F minor tonality for a series of variations which employ all musical style characteristics in a most successful correspondence to the verbal structures. The death in Berners Street, a gloomy but respectable professional and residential section, is portrayed by broad, accented vocal lines, and a nervous, menacing accompaniment in staccato chords (see Ex. 1. 6). The gruesome, poverty-stricken Houndsditch death in which

"There came to lay me out
A washerwoman and a witch"

17

Example 1.6, measures 5-12. Copyright © 1947, G. Schirmer, Inc.; used by permission.

receives an increasingly chromatic harmonic treatment, climaxing in loud, percussive, keyboard dissonances.

Example 1.7, measures 27-30. Copyright © 1947, G. Schirmer, Inc.; used by permission.

Holborn, a residential area embodying faded wealth and position, is musically suggested in pompous, legato vocal phrases, emphasized by the accompaniment's octave doublings, all in a meno mosso tempo. The solitary Marylebone episode, one of the most chilling, prefigures the terrifying dirge in Benjamin Britten's Serenade for tenor and horn. In a funeral march tempo, with low, underlying dissonances in the piano part, the vocal line rises from a portentous Phrygian second step to a horror-stricken climax an octave above. Notice that the dramatic emotion is intensified by the indicated decrescendo on the word "alone" in which a shriek is transformed into a whisper.

18

Example 1.8, measures 49-57. Copyright © 1947, G. Schirmer, Inc.; used by permission.

Death near Lincoln's Inn, surrounded by acquisitive relatives, takes on a *vivace* tempo as their chattering occasions a rapidly repeating pianistic figure. In the final stanza, Elinor Wylie describes what one senses as her ideal death, in Bloomsbury: a pleasant area of late eighteenth-century houses near the British museum that has been a literary district during the nineteenth and twentieth centuries. Mary Howe invests this death, occurring peacefully and beautifully "in the bend of your arm," with a turn to the parallel major key, diatonic harmony, and a flowing melodic line. The musical-theater flavor of the non-chord tones introduced in the final cadence aptly suggests the warmth of the surroundings, while the voice trails off on the dominant as though on an arrested breath (see Ex. 1.9).

"A Strange Story" appeared in Trivial Breath, a collection of poetry published in 1928, the last year of Elinor Wylie's life. It is not beyond the realm of possibility that the writer, with an impending sense of her own end and in-

19

Example 1.9, measures 97-108. Copyright © 1947, G. Schirmer, Inc.; used by permission.

creasing personal ties to England, morbidly imagined possible death scenes in the great city of London. Sadly, Destiny did not cooperate, and she died in a New York City apartment, far from Bloomsbury and the beloved presence.

Two more Howe-Wylie songs worthy of note appear in the Galaxy publications of 1959. The first, "Fair Annet's Song," is in Volume II (English Songs: Part 1). It sets a poem by the same name from Angels and Earthly Creatures (1929) which is a brief, poignant, eight-line statement of the impermanence of beauty and the consequent need to live in the present moment. Mary Howe's increasingly rich harmonic palette underlines the ambivalent, barely repressed anxiety of the text, and the attenuated note values intensify the final rise to a despairing vocal climax.

"Prinkin' Leddie,"[22] from Volume VII (English Songs:

Part 3), also keeps the same title as the 1921 poem from Nets to Catch the Wind. In this song, Mary Howe, whose ancestry was part Scottish, was not surprisingly drawn to set verses in which Elinor Wylie imitated the Scottish ballads that she had loved in childhood. There are many folk-derived elements in this vigorous setting: the accented 6/8 meter, the dotted note patterns, and the rapid thirty-second note keyboard figures which imitate a strummed instrument. The poetic theme, expressed by the "primping lady" (as the title translates), is the need for visual beauty to sustain us in the storms of life, and is no doubt one which had a strong appeal to the artist and the homemaker as well in both Mary Howe and Elinor Wylie.

Amy Lowell (1874-1925)

Amy Lowell was born into a family of illustrious Boston Brahmins descended from Percival Lowell, who had come to Newburyport in 1637. James Russell Lowell, the witty New England poet and first editor of the Atlantic Monthly, was her grandfather's cousin. Her brother Percival, an astronomer, proved the existence of the planet Pluto, and postulated the Martian "canals." Another brother, Abbot Lawrence Lowell, was president of Harvard, although he admitted to understanding little of his sister's poetry.

The poet was to express regret in subsequent years that she had received the private education of a young lady of fashion instead of being sent to a college or university like the male Lowells. It is perhaps true, as some critics have suggested, that her lack of academic training is apparent in her major critical studies such as the two volume biography of Keats published in the last year of her life.23 The precocious talent, however, was probably nurtured, as was Mary Howe's, by the lack of imposed scholastic structure, for at the early age of thirteen she contributed to a book (mostly written by her mother and older sister) which was published under the title Dream Drops or Stories from Fairy Land.

During her teens, Amy Lowell, who had fine features and an almost transparent skin, considered turning her talents toward the theater, but abandoned her hopes of being an

21

actress when a glandular disturbance caused her to gain weight excessively. She then tried writing for the stage, and when this failed also, she decided to be a poet. This long pilgrimage toward her most natural mode of expression explains why Amy Lowell's first book of poetry, A Dome of Many Coloured Glass, was published in 1912 when she was already 38 years old.

Having now turned her not inconsiderable energy and devotion to the poetic art, Lowell spent the next thirteen years of her life not only writing many volumes of her own poetry, but also engaging single-handedly in a massive public relations campaign in behalf of other writers. She wrote articles, books, reviews, and lectures on American poetry and helped start a series of anthologies that introduced Frost, Lindsay, Sandburg, Teasdale, Robinson, and Aiken to the public. She was also a staunch champion of new movements in poetic technique, and in 1913 went to England and took by storm the Imagist group of Lawrence, Pound, Fletcher, and H.D. When, on returning to America, she proceeded to publish Some Imagist Poets in three volumes that contained her own works as well, she was denounced as a usurper by Ezra Pound, who threatened suit.[24]

Indeed, an aura of controversy was never far from Amy Lowell, who was a central figure in the exciting meetings of the Poetry Society of America, founded in New York circa 1915. Colum describes her at the meetings as she "presented herself like a whirlwind and harangued the audience,"[25] and also recalls a lively incident at the MacDowell Club, when the poet, who had insisted on reading last (after Elinor Wylie and a number of others), was then highly offended by the sparseness of the remaining audience.[26]

Amy Lowell's colorful legend was fostered by her cigar-smoking, her pet English sheep-dogs, her luxurious Boston mansion called Sevenels (for seven Lowells), and the strange work schedule by which she rose at 3 P.M., dined at 8, and wrote from midnight to 6 A.M. Those who knew her were also quick to point out her kind heart and willingness to do battle for an artistic cause. One senses from the Herculean labors that probably shortened her life, a desperate need for accomplishment, perhaps as a substitute for the relationships largely denied her by her physical form. From the elegance and passion of her poetry, one gleans, also, a sense of an inner world far different from the aggressive coarseness of manner which she assumed, and behind which she hid her disappointments.

22

The "Three Hokku"27 which appear in Mary Howe's
English Songs: Part 2 (Volume VI of the Galaxy series) are
settings drawn from Lowell's poetry collection What's O'clock?
This collection, published in 1925, won the Pulitzer Prize
posthumously, in 1926, and concludes with "Lilacs," proba-
bly Amy Lowell's best-known poem and her favorite of all her
own lyrics. The three brief verses are numbers I, XIII, and
XXII from "Twenty-Four Hokku on a Modern Theme" and have
been set exactly as written, except for omission of capitals
beginning the second poetic line in numbers two and three.
Amy Lowell's strong interest in Oriental poetry, much in
vogue during her working years, had already been demon-
strated by Fir Flower Tablets (1921), a volume of poetry she
had translated and adapted from the Chinese, together with
Florence Ayscough. In "Twenty-Four Hokku" she essayed the
compressed Japanese poetic form which has become, in this
century, such an appealing medium to western poets practic-
ing verbal condensation, and to composers inspired by the
musical challenge. We find Mary Howe responding to this
challenge as she submits her naturally more expansive style
to the discipline of compression (each song is one page long).

The "modern theme" of Amy Lowell's title is clearly
the death of love, and the twenty-four verses suggest the poet
purging her grief by writing through the night. With the dawn
she sees her garden and looks for comfort from the "cold-
coloured flowers." Each of the verses Mary Howe chose to
set centers around one of these flower images, and each con-
trasts human emotion with the appearance of nature: a time-
honored poetic stance that is as familiar in the German lied
as in the much earlier Oriental lyrics. In number one, a
statement of gratitude for the unchanging beauty of the lark-
spur in a world of shifting relationships, Howe uses harmonic
means to portray the text. A basic E-flat tonality takes on

Example 1.10, measures 1-7. Copyright 1959, Galaxy Music
Corporation; used by permission.

"uncertainty" through chromatic neighbors and passing tones in the piano introduction (see Ex. 1.10). The vocal line enters on E-flat scale tones and flowers to a lyrical climax on "heavenly blue," supported by clear E-flat harmonies. Thereafter, a hint of the opening chromaticism begins to return, and pervades the quiet, closing piano chords, revealing that the promise of the larkspur is not quite enough to dispel the muted anguish of loss.

Example 1.11, measures 15-31.   Copyright 1959, Galaxy Music Corporation; used by permission.

Number two asks the question "How am I worthy?" in comparison with the grace and delicacy of the blooming iris. The pleasure that the poet feels in contemplating the iris turns to pain with the realization that her own outward form has been found wanting.   Mary Howe finds the perfect musical counterpart for the poetic idea in the harmonic device of pan-diatonicism. [28]   She begins the song by clearly establishing the key of D minor, but, even before the voice enters, has already begun to bring in elements of D-flat major which is the key of the entire vocal line (see Ex. 1.12).   The accompaniment continues to express elements of both D and D-flat to the end of the song, in a dualism that mirrors the conflicting emotions of the text.

24

Example 1.12, measures 1-13. Copyright 1959, Galaxy Music Corporation; used by permission.

Example 1.13, measures 15-19. Copyright 1959, Galaxy Music Corporation; used by permission.

In number three, the poet, blinded by a "night of labour" described in the previous verse, sees a vision in the garden which could be either "a cloud of lilies" or the form of the lost love. Once again, chordal treatment, combined this time with pianistic timbre, is the element which creates a coloristic correspondence to the pallid images of the poetry. An Impressionistic pedal point on F, with changing harmonies above, produces a blur of sound, like the blurred vision of

25

the poet. The pedal point also lends an obsessive quality to the setting, while reminiscences of the pandiatonic D and D-flat link it musically to the former one. It is as though love has produced a dizzying of the senses (see Ex. 1. 13).

Beside the richness of Mary Howe's harmonic scheme in these songs, other stylistic elements remain relatively unobtrusive. Dynamics are subdued, the vocal lines stay mostly within the range of a fourth or fifth, and the metric schemes are regular and inflexible throughout. Only the colors, it seems, are allowed to blend and mingle. Finally, it should be noted that these remarkable songs bear a dedication to Adele Addison, the soprano who figured in performances of many important contemporary works such as Copland's Emily Dickinson songs and Lukas Foss's Time Cycle.

Virgil Thomson (1896-   )
Marianne Moore (1887-1972)

The birthplace of Virgil Thomson was Kansas City, Missouri, which, in 1896, was a city having a rich cultural life, yet with sufficient rural atmosphere to provide a pleasant, "neighborhood" setting for a growing child. The young Thomson started musical studies at five, and early began performing on piano and organ to the encouragement of a large, family audience, despite his father's total lack of musical endowment. The composer has expressed pride in his southern forbears and in the fact that "the loyalties formed in my pre-adolescent years ... are to music, companionship, and hospitality. The hospitality," he says, "stems from central Missouri, which was my father's home, and from northern Kentucky, my mother's. Also from a legendary Virginia, as known through my grandmother and her brothers.[29] From this classical mid-South, seemingly so gentle, came my arrogance and my unhesitating disobedience."[30]

His developing skills and the assertive self-confidence whose genesis Thomson so aptly describes, led him to a church organist position at the age of twelve, the same year in which he was to compose his first songs. A literary talent surfaced early as well, and while attending Kansas City Junior College, the composer founded a magazine and formed a literary society. His education was interrupted by World War I, in which he served as a radio engineer appointed to

26

the school of Military Aeronautics at the University of Texas in Austin. The war ended, he completed Kansas City Junior College and departed for Harvard University.

Not surprisingly, Virgil Thomson was quickly integrated into the musical life of Harvard, both as an undergraduate member of the glee club, concertizing in Europe in the summer of 1921, and eventually as an instructor, after graduating in 1923. Nevertheless, the Northeast was an alien environment to him, and he never felt at home in Boston where "no one expands; the inhabitants seem rather to aim at compressing one another" by means of "wary eyes and necks that never turned around."[31]

Although uneasy in the environment, Virgil Thomson continued his musical enfolding at Harvard as he studied organ with Wallace Goodrich[32] and formed a deep appreciation of French music in courses with Edward Burlingame Hill. Sensing his imminent need of the language, he tutored with a cultured Parisian settled in Boston in return for piano lessons, so that he could "learn to speak French impeccably."[33] Following the Harvard Glee Club tour of 1921, he was able to remain in Paris for a year's study with Nadia Boulanger, as a result of a fellowship grant. On returning to the United States, he completed his Bachelor's degree and spent a postgraduate year instructing at Harvard and writing articles on music for Vanity Fair. With the five hundred dollars saved from the year's work, he set sail once again for his beloved France, to launch his life as a composer.

As Thomson himself describes it, when he left America in 1925, he abandoned blooming careers as an organist, teacher, and conductor. Nor was he ever again to write for Vanity Fair, The New Republic, or American Mercury, though all wanted pieces from him, as did The Dial's new editor, Marianne Moore.[34] In Paris, he could singlemindedly devote himself to composing, nurtured by the Gallic understanding of the necessity for involving all the faculties in the creative process. From ancestors who were mostly farmers, rather than shopkeepers or bankers, Thomson had apparently inherited the fortitude needed to depend on Providence in lieu of financial planning, and for the next eight years he lived on the support of patrons and an occasional fee or commission for music. The lively artistic life of Paris in the twenties proved to be an entirely natural milieu for his talent, urbanity, and gregariousness. Drawn quickly into the inner circles inhabited by Satie and "Les Six," Picasso, Gide, Coc-

27

teau, Hemingway, Fitzgerald, and Gertrude Stein, Virgil
Thomson settled down in 1927 at "numéro 17 quai Voltaire"
and remained there until World War II.

While living in Paris in the thirties, Thomson's liter-
ary leanings had resurfaced and he had become a correspond-
ent for Modern Music (the journal of the New York League of
Composers). During this period, he also wrote articles and
a book called The State of Music which was published in 1939
and reissued in 1962.35 It was not surprising, then, that on
his return to America he succeeded Lawrence Gilman as mu-
sic critic for the New York Herald Tribune, holding the post
until 1954. Many of his reviews, particularly from the pe-
riod 1944-1947, were collected in The Art of Judging Music36
and a number of these pieces are relevant to this study. Of
particular interest are programs and reviews of New York
voice recitals37 and articles entitled "Singing Today" and "The
American Song." In the sixties, Virgil Thomson rejoined the
academic world as visiting professor at the University of Buf-
falo and Andrew Mellon professor at Carnegie Tech, also pub-
lishing his memoirs, Virgil Thomson, in 1967.38 He con-
tinued to live in the Chelsea hotel overlooking southern New
York City which had been his American home since 1940, and
a television interview in the fall of 1980 showed views of this
apartment as well as of 17 quai Voltaire in Paris. With
eighty-four years behind him, most of them spent in the fore-
front of the musical world on two continents, Virgil Thomson
affirmed to the viewing audience that he didn't believe in re-
gretting things. "The outcome of anything or the way it hap-
pened," said he, "is the story of your life."

A year later, in October of 1981, the author met Mr.
Thomson while he was attending a performance of The Mother
of Us All in San Antonio, Texas. Although somewhat hard of
hearing on that occasion, Thomson retained his lifelong ele-
gance, wit, and keen-edged intelligence, together with a lack
of pretentiousness that made him prefer to be addressed as
"Mister" despite his admittedly numerous honorary doctoral
degrees. In discussing the various forms of his vocal writing,
he expressed the opinion that one "works out difficulties in
small pieces," i.e. songs, so that in the writing of "big
pieces" (operas) one doesn't have to worry about technique,
but he stressed that he had found each form to be uniquely
challenging.

This devotion of Virgil Thomson to the vocal forms
of composition is demonstrated by the fact that he began his

composing career while still at Harvard with a choral piece, De Profundis, and a song called "Vernal Equinox" to an Amy Lowell text. (Thomson as an undergraduate was evidently in touch with the most recent directions in American poetry, for Lowell's work had begun to be published only a few years before he entered Harvard.) As time went on, he became increasingly committed to solving the problems of musical declamation in the English language, which he felt had hardly been addressed. His collaborations with Gertrude Stein in the operas Four Saints in Three Acts and The Mother of Us All were particularly pertinent to this purpose, and critical estimation of his success is aptly voiced by Victor Yellin: "Virgil Thomson's main contribution to American music is his blending of the musical elements of melody, harmony, and rhythm into a musical style proper to American speech. "39

Thomson's place as a major contributor to and spokesman for twentieth-century American music is undisputed. Marianne Moore holds a similar position in her art form, and had become a revered "high priestess" of American poetry some thirty years before her death at the age of eighty-five. She was born in a suburb of St. Louis, Missouri, which was the home of her grandfather, the Reverend John R. Warner. Her mother had returned there from Massachusetts after her husband, a construction engineer, suffered a mental breakdown from which he never recovered. Marianne Moore never knew her father, but had an older brother who was later to enter the ministry, and the two children remained very close to each other and to their mother, Mary Warner Moore, all their lives. Mrs. Moore was an English teacher who imposed the strictest standards of behavior on herself and her children. The poet acknowledged the profound influence of this early training while admitting that she had experienced it as overly rigorous.

When Moore was seven years old her grandfather died, and the family moved to Carlisle, Pennsylvania, where she attended the Metzger Elementary School and the Metzger Institute, a secondary school for girls. In 1905 she entered Bryn Mawr College, and these formative undergraduate years were to provide both discouragement and support to the fledgling writer. The often-quoted English composition teacher's criticism, "I presume you had an idea, if one could find out what it is, " drove her for a time into science courses where she developed precision of thinking and economy of expression. These qualities served her well on her return to literature, and she began to publish poems in Tipyn O'Bob, the campus

29

magazine, and in the Lantern (Bryn Mawr's alumnae monthly) after her graduation in 1909.

In 1911, Marianne Moore began a five year stint on the faculty of the United States Indian School in Carlisle. Then she and her mother moved to Chatham, New Jersey, to be with her brother who had been made pastor of Ogden Memorial Church. The next move, two years later, was to Greenwich Village. Here she became a leading figure in a lively literary circle which included Wallace Stevens and William Carlos Williams. The poet, with her mother, left the Village in 1929 (the year of The Dial's demise) for Brooklyn, where her brother was serving as chaplain at the Navy Yard. She returned to Greenwich Village thirty-six years later by herself (her mother having died in 1947) because of Brooklyn's rising crime rate, and it was to be her last move.

During the half century of Marianne Moore's life in the New York area, she supported herself in a number of ways, which included private school teaching, working in the New York Public Library system, editing The Dial (1926-1929), acting as poet-in-residence at colleges such as Bryn Mawr (1953) and Barnard (late fifties),[40] and eventually receiving numerous prizes and fellowships as well as royalties on her many published volumes of poetry, essays, and translations. Her influence on her poetic contemporaries during the formative decade of the twenties was profound, as is evidenced by William Carlos Williams' description of her in his autobiography: "a rafter holding up the superstructure of our uncompleted building, a caryatid, her red hair plaited and wound twice about the fine skull ... one of the main supports of the new order."[41] As time went on, the adulation of critics and other colleagues such as T. S. Eliot, Louis Untermeyer, and John Ashberry continued to proliferate, and by the end of her life she had received honorary degrees from nine colleges and universities, including N. Y. U. and Harvard, as well as Bryn Mawr's M. Carey Thomas award.

Marianne Moore felt a lasting debt of gratitude to Imagists such as T. S. Eliot and Ezra Pound who had had some of her early work published by the Egoist Press in London. Her own connection to Imagism has been alternately maintained and denied by critics. Most of them now agree that while her early poems follow the Imagist dictum of concentrating on objective data drawn from the natural environment, the later works increasingly incorporate Moore's affectionate but strongly ethical and value-oriented view of the world.

Her poetic language, which most commonly employs a syllabic form derived from French versification (in which accent plays little part), has been praised for its clarity and concision and, on occasion, damned for its awkwardness and obscurity.[42] A British critic, with the perspective of distance, has provided one of the most perceptive assessments of her work: "Unmistakably modern, she has no modern formlessness.... Her style, for all its asymmetry, is rapid, clear, unself-concerned, flexible, and accurate, and her work gradually discloses her exceptional sanity, intelligence, and imaginative depth."[43]

Virgil Thomson's connections with Marianne Moore had already begun when she had unsuccessfully solicited articles for The Dial from him in the mid-twenties. He was shortly thereafter to have considerable contact with her poetry through an interesting coincidence. In 1928, Thomson left Paris for a visit to the United States and stayed for a time in Massachusetts with Jessie Lasell, a woman who enjoyed reading aloud from the works of Marianne Moore, among others of her favorite poets. It might also be mentioned that Mrs. Lasell's son-in-law was J. Sibley Watson who had revived The Dial as a literary monthly together with Scofield Thayer,[44] and who had held the managing editorship just before Marianne Moore.[45] In later years, the independently wealthy Watson and his wife, Hildegarde, were to include Ms. Moore in a group of occasionally impoverished literary friends to whom they served as benefactors.[46]

It seems not at all surprising that Thomson would have, in time, been drawn to musical setting of some of Moore's texts, considering their mutually strong endowments in the areas of humor, sophistication, fondness for verbal sound manipulation, and preference for apparent simplicity over deliberate complexity. (Thomson had come to this preference in the process of turning away from "self-indulgent" German music[47] toward the restraint of the French, while with Moore it was the "modernist" reaction against nineteenth-century poetic romanticism.) Interestingly, however, it was at the suggestion of Marianne Moore that Thomson wrote "English Usage" and "My Crow Pluto"[48] and she herself who chose for setting these two poems which had originally borne the titles "I've Been Thinking" and "To Victor Hugo of My Crow Pluto."[49]

Mr. Thomson described the incident in these terms: "I knew Marianne Moore for twenty or thirty years, and although she never had anyone over, she would come to my place now and then for lunch. On one occasion, she brought along these two poems and said 'I thought you might like to set these to music.' I replied 'They're very difficult--I think I will.'" Thomson added that he was referring not to a difficulty of meaning but of prosody, and that he felt impelled to rise to the challenge.[50]

It is indeed true that most of Marianne Moore's poetry consists of lines with varying numbers of syllables and accents, very infrequent rhymes, and a highly flexible, nonprosodic flow. It is a style that has apparently proved forbidding to song composers who, despite Moore's towering reputation, have, to this date, set little of her poetry. The two poems which she selected for Virgil Thomson, however, are somewhat different. They are both written in short-line couplets, which mostly rhyme in "I've Been Thinking," and terminate in complementary "o" or "oo" vowel sounds throughout in "To Victor Hugo." Verbal accent patterns are fairly regular, also, and it is possible to see why these tighter structures were judged by the poet to be more appropriate to the musical medium, while still presenting as "difficult" to the composer in their distortions of the traditional rhythms of American speech.

"I've Been Thinking" appears in Moore's Complete Poems (published in 1967, her eightieth year) under the section heading "Hitherto Uncollected." Three small but interesting changes in the poem are to be found in Thomson's setting. In the seventeenth couplet he adds "eh?" after "I've escaped?" to make the question more emphatic. In couplet twenty-one he uses "Afric" instead of "capric," a change so major that one must assume the original as printed had been an error, now restored according to the poet's intent. Thirdly, the song carries a period rather than a colon after the line "I'm sure of this," which serves to link it to the former idea ("Not verse/Of course") rather than to the following one ("Nothing mundane is divine;/Nothing divine is mundane.") In this case, since the colon carries forward the poem's train of thought and the period does not, it seems likely that the period was an error in the music printing (see Example 1.16).

As already indicated, the title, too, has been changed from the ambiguous "I've Been Thinking" to the particular "English Usage." Actually, it is a very specific type of English usage that Moore satirizes and repudiates in this poem: the affected, upper class, pseudo-British speech that

32

she possibly first encountered at Bryn Mawr College,[51] which typically overuses such epithets as "divine," "frightful," "enchanting," and the like. With characteristic intellectual honesty, however, the poet admits that the whimsical couplets in which she has expressed her contempt, are themselves a form of the very same "word diseases" as the affected speech syndrome. Having confessed this, she plays with the sound of words, parodying her own verse form ("Attic/Afric-Alcaic"), then ends the frivolity as becomes her, with a moral statement indicating the real reason for her objection to at least one of the above epithets (i.e., "Nothing mundane is divine;").

So great is Virgil Thomson's mastery of musical declamation and the rhythm of language that he has frequently been known to improvise settings at the piano following the text on his music rack.[52] "English Usage" has some of that spontaneous quality, and the vocal line is primary throughout, with the piano supplying a supportive background of punctuating parallel chords. The most striking rhythmic aspect of this setting is the fact that Thomson has, in effect, destroyed the prosody of Moore's verse as written and has, instead, gone back to the more natural accent pattern of the lines as they would sound if spoken. In so doing, he has achieved the "solution," as it were, to the prosodic difficulties which he perceived as the original challenge.

33

Example 1.14, measures 1-8. Copyright © 1966, G. Schirmer, Inc.; used by permission.

The vocal line is non-lyric, and the many chordal leaps seem appropriate to the rapid and capricious leaping about from one verbal idea to another that occurs in the poem. The vocal line also shows a clear allegiance to the key of G major, with only occasional chromatic alterations. However, the accompanying chords, always in the cheerful major mode, seem to be applied vertically to the needs of the individual melody notes, rather than being governed by the horizontal demands of harmonic necessity. This serves to reinforce the disjointed, leaping melodic contour mentioned above (see Ex. 1.15).

To underline Marianne Moore's closing defense of divinity, Thomson provides a piano interlude of mock portent, and changes to a broad triplet pattern observed by both voice and piano. Because of the similar rhythmic movement, a polytonal feeling is created by the juxtaposition of the G major vocal line and the accompanying B-flat and A major elements. The effect of these musical devices is to suggest that a basically serious statement is being held up to good-humored self-parody (see Ex. 1.16).

The poem "To Victor Hugo of My Crow Pluto," together with an explanatory essay ("My Crow Pluto-a Fantasy"), was published in 1966 in the collection Tell Me, Tell Me, 53 but had originally appeared in Harper's Bazaar of October, 1961. Ironically, Tell Me, Tell Me also contained an essay called "A Burning Desire to Be Explicit" in which Moore decries the charge of obscurity which clings to her despite her constant efforts at clarity: a charge that has

Example 1.15, measures 24-28. Copyright © 1966, G. Schirmer, Inc.; used by permission.

Peterborough, N. H., August 8, 1965

Example 1.16, measures 34-41. Copyright © 1966, G. Schirmer, Inc.; used by permission.

certainly been leveled, in some circles, at the "Pluto" writings.[54]

Part of the problem turns on the poet's erudition, which Babette Deutsch describes in these terms: ". . . the mental acquisitiveness that furnishes her verse with some of its most remarkable details, sometimes turns it into a bibliographical curiosity."[55] Moore's dedication of this poem to Victor Hugo, which formed part of the original title, is fairly easily understood; in couplets five through eight she agrees with the Hugo quotation set above the poem (and the song) which suggests that the winged spirit of her crow is indeed apparent, "even when the bird is walking." Thereafter, however, the need for explanatory notes increases, as Moore begins to feed in snatches of what she calls a "pseudo esperanto, " and which she translates at the end of her poem, as the song's publishers unfortunately do not. The story of her relationship with the crow who adopted her is clearly set forth in the essay, which, in this writer's opinion, should also have been printed with the song, in the fashion of some of the notes and quotations attendant on Charles Ives' song publications. Plato, we discover in the essay, was a verbal variant of her name for him, as well as a judgment of his qualities. "Lucro è peso morto" ("Profit is a dead weight") is an Italian phrase found in the poem's eighteenth couplet, and is also the title of another of Moore's essays. Her strong conviction on this point, she tells us, made her uneasy with the spoils of the crow's skillful thievery. The end of the story, which is clear from the poem as well as the essay, was her return of the bird to natural woodland, not without regret for the loss of a handsome and large-spirited companion.

Perhaps the reason that Virgil Thomson was not concerned about detailed explanations of this somewhat puzzling verbal material is to be found in his own statement concerning English musical declamation. It was made in regard to his collaborations with Gertrude Stein, but is directly appropriate to this situation as well. "My theory was, " he says, "that if a text is set correctly for the sound of it, the meaning will take care of itself. . . . With meanings . . . abstracted, or absent, or so multiplied that choice among them is impossible, there is no temptation toward tonal illustration, say, of birdie babbling by the brook or heavy hangs my heart."[56] In these terms, Thomson underlines his fundamental opposition to the musically descriptive German lied approach to vocal writing, and indeed, the Moore settings seem rather to derive from the composer's lifelong Gallic devotion. They not only express an insouciance reminiscent of his (by then) forty year old Dadaist connection, but are also dedicated to the memory of Francis Poulenc, a leading member of "Les Six" who had died in 1962, just one year before these songs were written.

There are two levels, then, of meaning in this song, and interestingly, the setting works on both of them. On the first level, we find a structure in which merely the sound of the words has been joined to accompaniment so as to create a musically satisfying experience. The piano writing is much more linear here than in "English Usage," and the legato lines of the keyboard mirror the liquid sound of all the "o" and "oo" rhymes as well as the Italianate flow of the "esperanto madinusa" (made in U. S. A.) as Moore calls it.

Example 1.17, measures 1-7. Copyright © 1966, G. Schirmer, Inc.; used by permission.

Supporting rhythmic patterns are grouped into a skillful three-part form, in which the piano at first mimics the voice's quarter- and eighth-note narrative (see Example 1.17), then breaks up into the greater urgency of sixteenth-note arpeggios,

37

Example 1.18, measures 15-16. Copyright © 1966, G. Schirmer, Inc.; used by permission.

and ends with staccato and syncopated eighths and quarters in a continuing crescendo of rhythmic excitement.

Example 1.19, measures 36-38. Copyright © 1966, G. Schirmer, Inc.; used by permission.

Adding to the build-up of musical tension is the gradually increasing dynamic level which opens at a modest piano and ends fortissimo with the steepest ascent in the last section (see Example 1.19).

On the second level, with our informed understanding of the dramatic elements of the text, we can begin to view the soft, legato opening with accompaniment doubling the voice line, as a thoughtful and wryly affectionate reminiscence (see Example 1.17). Agitation mounts in section two as the poet brings the relationship more vividly to mind, recalling their private language and the looting which enforced their separation. Section three is now seen as an exaggerated tribute to

38

the wild beauty and nobility of the bird, with the final "addio"
backed by a rush of ascending whole-tone scales in a parodied
wail of grief.

Example 1.20, measures 42-47. Copyright © 1966, G. Schir-
mer, Inc.; used by permission.

NOTES

1. Madeleine Goss, Modern Music Makers (New York: E. P. Dutton, 1952), p. 71.

2. Conversation with Calderon Howe, M.D., on May 24, 1981. Dr. Howe, who is Mary Howe's son, retired in 1982 as Chairman of the Department of Microbiology at Louisiana State University in New Orleans. He currently resides in Newport, R.I.

3. Ibid. Dr. Howe added that his mother's only conflict between her work and family life had arisen in the thirties, when Mary Howe's mother's protracted illness made the composer reluctant to fulfill her out-of-town commitments.

4. Goss, pp. 71-72.

5. As a further sidelight on her academic career, it should be noted that Mary Howe received an honorary degree from George Washington University in 1961.

6. Goss includes a fairly complete catalog of Howe's works up to 1950 (pp. 78-82). The principal compositions beyond that date are the seven volumes of songs (see note #8).

7. Calderon Howe interview.

8. New York: Galaxy Music Corp., 1959.

9. Mary Colum, Life and the Dream (Garden City, N.Y.: Doubleday, 1947), p. 338. The MacDowell Club readings are one among many invaluable pieces of information in this book relating to American literary life ca. 1914-1940. Mary Colum, herein writing her memoirs, was the wife of Padraic Colum, the Irish author, and an editor and literary critic in her own right.

10. Colum describes an agonizing occasion at an English country house when a fellow guest recognized Elinor and Horace and reported on the scandal surrounding them to the hostess (p. 337). Commenting on the poet's lifelong praise of Horace Wylie's personal qualities, Colum says "a man who could throw his life away for love, flinging prudence to the wind, is rare anywhere, and almost impossible in that period in America, so I am inclined to credit Elinor's vision of him." (p. 341).

40

11. Stanley Olson, Elinor Wylie, A Life Apart (New York: Dial, 1979). Olson takes a different view of Wylie. He sees him as a charming but rather weak man, with an impetuous and changeable nature.

12. For further material on Douglas Moore see Chapter 4, Volume I of this study (American Art Song and American Poetry). Edna St. Vincent Millay is discussed in Chapter 2 of the present volume.

13. Mary Howe, "Spring Pastoral" (New York: G. Schirmer, 1936). The manuscript of the orchestral version is in the New York Public Library at Lincoln Center. Mary Howe, "Robin Hood's Heart" (unpublished).

14. Mary Howe, "Little Elegy" (New York: G. Schirmer, 1939). Medium voice. Range: e^1 to e^2. Mary Howe, "When I Died in Berners Street" (New York: G. Schirmer, 1947). Medium high voice. Range: c^1 to g-flat^2. Mary Howe, "Let Us Walk in the White Snow" (New York: Carl Fischer, 1948). Medium high voice. Range: d^1 to g^2. All three of the above are now out of print in the original editions. "Let Us Walk in the White Snow" has been reprinted in Contemporary Songs in English edited by Bernard Taylor (New York: Carl Fischer, 1956). The other two are available from the music collection of the New York Public Library at Lincoln Center, and G. Schirmer has indicated its willingness to make special reprints of out-of-print songs on request.

15. Thomas A. Gray, Elinor Wylie (New York: Twayne, 1969), p. 49.

16. The string quartet setting is available on rental from G. Schirmer, Inc.

17. See American Art Song and American Poetry, Volume I, Chapter 1, p. 16.

18. Ibid.

19. This string quartet setting is available on rental from Carl Fischer, Inc. The manuscript is held by the Library of Congress, Washington, D.C., and the New York Public Library has a photostat.

20. Gray, p. 50.

21. Colum, p. 364.

22. "Fair Annet's Song" and "Prinkin' Leddie" are both for medium high voice. The range in each case is c^1 to g^2.

23. Colum, p. 252.

24. The major source of the foregoing biographical material is Louis Untermeyer's introduction to Amy Lowell, The Complete Poetical Works (Boston: Houghton Mifflin, 1955), pp. xxi-xxix.

25. Colum, p. 251.

26. Ibid., p. 338.

27. Medium high voice. Range: g^1 to g^2.

28. Pan-diatonicism is the use of step-wise, adjacent tonal centers. It was a harmonic device frequently employed by Igor Stravinsky.

29. One of Virgil Thomson's ancestors had helped to found the colony of Jamestown, Virginia.

30. Virgil Thomson, Virgil Thomson (New York: Knopf, 1967), p. 18.

31. Ibid., p. 48.

32. Wallace Goodrich or "Goody," as he was affectionately known to many Harvard and Radcliffe undergraduates, had a long, fruitful teaching career. This writer remembers, in her own undergraduate days at Bryn Mawr College, "Goody" coming along with the Harvard Glee Club on their trip to Bryn Mawr for a joint concert in 1946.

33. Kathleen Hoover and John Cage, Virgil Thomson, His Life and Music (Freeport, N.Y.: Books for Libraries Press, 1959), p. 34.

34. Thomson, p. 73.

35. Published by Henry Holt and Co.

36. Published by Alfred A. Knopf, 1948.

37. A review entitled "Pretty Singing" (p. 83) prints the program of a recital by Muriel Rahn. Included are two songs

by William Grant Still, "Winter's Approach" and "Breath of a Rose," both of which are discussed in Chapter 4, Volume I of American Art Song and American Poetry.

38. See note #30.

39. Victor Yellin, "The Operas of Virgil Thomson," American Music Since 1910, ed. Virgil Thomson (New York: Holt, Rinehart and Winston, 1971), p. 91. In this same collection, there is a very interesting essay by Thomson himself called "American Musical Traits" which traces the ethnic derivations of style characteristics such as melody, rhythm, and dynamics.

40. Ms. Natalie Beller, a San Antonio singer and voice teacher, who received her B. A. from Barnard College in 1959, has vivid recollections of Marianne Moore's warmth and energy during the poetry readings she held on campus. Personal recollections of Ms. Moore at a slightly earlier period (i.e. in the thirties and forties) are presented at some length in the following memoir: Elizabeth Bishop, "Efforts of Affection," Vanity Fair, 46: 4 (June 1983), pp. 44-61.

41. William Carlos Williams, Autobiography (New York: Random House, 1951), p. 146.

42. Some of the outstanding critical studies on Marianne Moore are:
   a) Bernard F. Engel, Marianne Moore (New York: Twayne, 1964).
   b) George Nitchie, Moore: An Introduction to the Poetry (New York: Columbia University Press, 1969).
   c) Pamela White Hadas, Moore: Poet of Affection (Syracuse, N.Y.: Syracuse University Press, 1977).

43. M. J. Alexander, "Marianne Moore," Great Writers of the English Language--Poets, ed. James Vinson (New York: St. Martin's, 1979), p. 710.

44. Mary Colum has much to say concerning Scofield Thayer's nobility of character, coupled with a nervous instability that led eventually to a breakdown. One moving passage (p. 384) describes his generous handling of a desperate request for funds sent by James Joyce to the Colums after the start of World War I.

45. Most of the foregoing information in this paragraph comes from Thomson, Chapter 13, ("American Interlude").

46. Virgil Thomson in the San Antonio interview, October 4, 1981. He added that Marianne Moore, "an odd woman," was not as poor as she seemed, and at her death surprised everyone by leaving a sizable sum of money to her nephew.

47. Thomson, p. 117.

48. a) Virgil Thomson, "English Usage" (New York: G. Schirmer, 1966). Medium voice. Range: d^1 to e^2. b) Virgil Thomson, "My Crow Pluto" (New York: G. Schirmer, 1966). Medium high voice. Range: d^1 to f^2. Both of these songs have been recorded by Meriel and Peter Dickinson, a British singer and pianist. The record, titled An American Anthology, is under the Unicorn label, distributed in this country by Euroclass in New York City.

49. The information contained in the foregoing sentence comes from a letter written by Virgil Thomson to the author, dated September 30, 1980.

50. San Antonio interview.

51. Forty years later, during the author's years at Bryn Mawr College (see note #31), this type of speech affectation was still widely encountered.

52. Yellin, p. 95.

53. Published by Viking Press.

54. See Nitchie, p. 150.

55. Babette Deutsch, Poetry in Our Time (Garden City, N.Y.: Doubleday, 1963), p. 229.

56. Thomson, Virgil Thomson, p. 90.

II. JOHN DUKE I (1899-   )

Adelaide Crapsey (1878-1914), Edna St. Vincent Millay (1892-1950), Edwin Arlington Robinson (1869-1935), Elinor Wylie (1885-1928).

"Fifty years from now, John Duke is going to be known as the representative figure of his era in American song-writing." This statement was made to the author by John Seagle,[1] who, as director since 1947 of the Seagle summer vocal colony[2] at Schroon Lake, New York, has been actively involved with American singers and composers of vocal literature for almost forty years. An equally impressive accolade comes from the pen of the redoubtable Virgil Thomson. After lamenting the generally sorry state of the American art song in a 1947 critical essay,[3] Mr. Thomson ended his review of a Povla Frisch recital the following year by remarking that "John Duke's 'Bells in the Rain' was the only song that stood up as workmanship beside the Poulenc pieces."[4]

There is no doubt that John Duke has made one of the major contributions of this century to the growing body of American art songs. His catalog to date (published and unpublished)[5] shows a staggering total of two hundred and fifty-two settings,[6] which cover an extremely wide range of poetic subject matter and musical treatment. Yet a paradox surrounds this man who has devoted a long, vigorous lifetime to the art of setting poetry to music, and it stems from the fact that it was not exactly what he had in mind. "I am still amazed," he wrote in 1981, "at the way my musical career has turned out. In my early days, my ambition was to be a great pianist, and I could not have believed anyone who told me I was destined to be a song composer."[7]

45

John Duke has lived in Massachusetts for well over half a century. Since 1964, his home has been a sunny, two-story, white frame house of comfortable proportions on tree-shaded Harrison Avenue in Northampton.[8] However, despite this typical New England setting in which he is now totally at home, Duke's origins are Southern, and a family legend claims that his paternal grandfather left Columbia, South Carolina, on the last train before Sherman burned the city. His father, Harry K. Duke, spent his youth in Charles Town, West Virginia, then moved to Cumberland, Maryland, where he engaged in various business ventures, including a book store. John Duke was born in Cumberland, and recalls "an almost ideal family life"[9] as the eldest of six children. His father had a strong interest in literature, and one of the composer's earliest memories is of hearing him read aloud famous passages from Shakespearean plays. Duke's mother, Matilda Hoffman, was a singer of some accomplishment, and an old photograph shows her playing the guitar, her preferred accompanying instrument. It was a household devoted to both words and music: the ideal nurturing ground for a song composer.

After learning to read music under his mother's instruction, John Duke began his formal study of the piano at the age of eleven, with a woman named Beatrice Holmes. He evidently made rapid progress, as a year later he was already playing the piano and organ in local church services. His most intensive training began when at sixteen he won a scholarship at the Peabody Conservatory in Baltimore. Here he was to remain for three years, climaxing his studies with a performance of the Saint-Saëns G minor concerto accompanied by the Conservatory orchestra.[10]

Peabody had been patterned by its founder after European models, and Duke's teachers were solidly grounded in nineteenth-century traditions. John Duke studied the piano with Harold Randolph who had himself been trained at Peabody by pupils of von Bülow, Clara Schumann, and Liszt. Randolph, a member of one of the "first families of Virginia" which had been impoverished by the Civil War, was a fine solo and ensemble pianist. He was also an able administrator, and built the Conservatory into an outstanding music school during his years as director. John Duke's mentor in composition was Gustav Strube, the "grand old man" of post-World War I music in Baltimore, who had been born in the Hartz mountains in Germany and had studied at the Leipzig Conservatory with Karl Reinecke before coming to this country.[11] Strube had also been Mary Howe's professor of composition,[12] but although she had taken her degree in 1922, just four years after Duke's graduation, their paths did not cross. "I don't remember ever meeting Mary Howe," writes John Duke, "although I was very well acquainted with her friend, Anne Hull, with whom she often gave two piano recitals."[13]

A period of volunteer service in the army during which he was stationed with the SATC at Columbia University brought the young musician to New York City. When World War I ended, he remained there to study the piano with Franklin Cannon (a Leschetizsky pupil) and composition under Howard Brockway and Bernard Wagenaar. Both of these composers possessed an active vocal orientation which no doubt strengthened the student's inclinations. Brockway, who had taught at Peabody before settling in New York, published two albums of Kentucky folk song settings in 1916 and 1920, which was in line with the growing interest of the era in indigenous musical material. Wagenaar, a native of Holland and only five years older than Duke, was also making a significant contribution to the art song at this time. In 1925 and 1928 (several years after Duke's period of study), he wrote song cycles to the poetry of Edna St. Vincent Millay, thus placing himself among the pioneers in the setting of contemporary American poetry, and prefiguring John Duke's Millay settings which began in 1935.

Between 1922 and 1923, Duke was employed in editing pianola rolls for the Ampico recording laboratories. It was while working on Artur Schnabel's recordings that a friendship was formed which later took him to Berlin to study with the world-famous pianist. Just before Christmas of 1922, John Duke married Dorothy Macon of Falls Church, Virginia, whose father was Capt. Edward N. Macon of the U.S. Army and whose brother, General Robert C. Macon, played a leading role in the final European campaign of World War II. This was the beginning of a long and devoted relationship[14] that was to become a professional partnership as well, for Mrs. Duke had reacted strongly against her military background when she found herself increasingly drawn toward literature and the arts. As a writer, she shared her husband's deep interest in poetry,[15] and in the course of time served as his librettist on several occasions.[16]

The year 1923 was an important one for John Duke, as it marked the beginning of a long teaching career at Smith

College during which he was to become Henry Dike Sleeper Professor of Music. The same year also saw the first appearance of his compositions in print, with G. Schirmer's publication of a piano work ("The Fairy Glen") and two songs ("I've Dreamed of Sunsets" and "Lullaby") which had been written in 1920 and 1921 respectively.[17] By now thoroughly settled in the academic way of life, Duke spent his first sabbatical leave (1929-30) in the European musical capitals of Berlin and Paris where he studied the piano with Schnabel and compositional analysis with Nadia Boulanger. The latter experience was to have an immediate, discernible effect on his composition, and many of his songs written in the 1930's show the combination of French and avant-garde influences together with a reaching out toward a unique personal style that was this creative teacher's legacy to all her students.

From 1930 until his retirement from Smith College in 1967 as professor emeritus, John Duke divided his activities into three principal categories: teaching, performing, and composing. Some of the highlights of his teaching career were a course on the "History of Technical Theory in Piano Playing" given for the University Extension in Springfield and Amherst; a series of lectures on "The Arts Today" in association with Oliver Larkin, given at the Smith Summer Session of 1944; and an address to the December 1954 National Association of Teachers of Singing convention in Chattanooga on the subject "A Composer Looks at Contemporary Song Literature," after which a program of his works was presented.

Also in 1954, Duke began his long and fruitful involvement with the Seagle Colony[18] where he continues each summer to preside over master classes in the performance of his works. This writer was fortunate enough to attend one of these sessions, held on July 31st, 1982, the day after John Duke's eighty-third birthday.[19] In the rustic but acoustically grateful wooden theater overlooking a hazy Schroon Lake, sixteen young singers performed Duke songs old and new, several of which were first performances. To each, the composer (who knows all the poetry he has set by heart and quotes it readily) stressed the importance of a meaningful reading of the poem as a prelude to successful interpretation of the song, and made other comments on tempi or rhythmic inaccuracies which most often related to verbal and poetic elements.

As a further result of this professional and personal association between Duke and the Seagle colony, the composer

48

arranged to spend his sabbatical year of 1955-56 as a visiting professor of piano at Trinity University in San Antonio, Texas, where John Seagle was professor of voice from 1947 to 1980. This appointment was in the nature of a homecoming for Mrs. Duke, who, because of her military background had from her girlhood various ties to Fort Sam Houston.

In the capacity of performing pianist, John Duke has presented innumerable concerts throughout his career. These have indicated a freely ranging musical curiosity and a particular interest in the American scene that began with his programming of MacDowell's Keltic Sonata on a number of recitals in the early twenties. For several summers he appeared as piano soloist and chamber player at the Yaddo summer colony of creative artists in Saratoga Springs, and in 1936, as executive chairman of the concert committee, was able to organize as well as participate in programs of contemporary American music. The Yaddo experience brought him into contact with such other American musicians and writers as Roy Harris, Ralph Kirkpatrick, and John Cheever, for that valuable cross-fertilization of ideas which is a principal "raison d'être" of the summer artists' colony.[20]

John Duke also gave many first performances of works by well-known American composers in New York, Boston, and Princeton as well as Saratoga Springs. One of these was the Roger Sessions Piano Sonata #1 which he premièred at one of the historic Copland-Sessions concerts of contemporary music.[21] Others included works by Walter Piston, Bernard Wagenaar (his former teacher), and the Piano Sonata #3 by Ross Lee Finney who was a colleague of Duke's at Smith College before his move to a position at the University of Michigan. By way of combining his interests in teaching and performing American piano literature, Duke presented numerous lecture-recitals through the years on the works of Louis Moreau Gottschalk.[22] In this undertaking he had the assistance of Dorothy Duke, who was also interested in the career of this colorful musician, and who collected material on Gottschalk for inclusion in a book which was completed, but not published.

A chronological survey of John Duke's compositional output to date shows a meaningful and increasing pull toward vocal forms. During the nineteen thirties and forties he produced nine major instrumental works, of which two were orchestral and seven for various chamber groups. Among performances of these, the following were notable: the String

49

Quartet played by the Walden and N.B.C. quartets; the Concerto for Piano and Strings performed over New York's WQXR in 1945; the String Trio played at a Yaddo festival; and the Carnival Overture performed by the Boston Pops Orchestra and the National Orchestra Association of New York.

In the nineteen fifties, Duke developed an "increasing interest in opera,"23 partly, no doubt, because of the performance opportunities provided by his newly formed association with the Seagle colony. In the summer of 1953, his first opera, Captain Lovelock, was performed at Schroon Lake. For this work, John Duke prepared his own libretto, which he adapted from a Danish play. In his second opera, The Sire de Maletroit's Door (1958), taken from a Robert Louis Stevenson story, he had the collaboration of Dorothy Duke as librettist. She had also filled a similar role in the composition of the 1944 Musical Fantasy for Children which was based on a Rudyard Kipling story, "The Cat That Walked by Himself."

The middle of the same decade (1955) saw the publication by G. Schirmer of "O, Sing Unto the Lord" for women's voices and string orchestra or organ, and Duke has also written five other choral works. But the overwhelming body of his composition, which he produced copiously during the decades of his involvement with other forms, and exclusively for the past twenty years, has been songs. Partly, perhaps, in the effort to explicate the power of his attraction toward this medium, and partly because the increased leisure afforded him the opportunity to write as well as compose, John Duke has, since his retirement, published two articles which rank as classics in the literature on song-writing: "Some Reflections on the Art Song in English"24 and "The Significance of Song."25 Also, since his retirement, Duke has continued to be involved throughout the country in recitals of his songs in which he serves as accompanist. The author was involved in one such occasion at Duke University in November, 1963, when she moderated a panel discussion on "Words and Music" which preceded a concert of Duke songs for soprano, baritone, and tenor.26 One of the most recent of similar events occurred in April, 1981, at the University of Maryland, when John Duke accompanied Phyllis Bryn-Julson, soprano, and Donald Boothman, baritone, in a program of his songs.

During the last fifteen years, a proliferation of John Duke recordings have made him even more widely known as

50

a composer and pianist. Volumes I and II of Art Song in America[27] contained five and three Duke songs respectively, performed by tenor John Hanks, who has headed the Duke University voice department since 1954. Hanks was closely associated with the composer during his six years at Smith College directly before coming to North Carolina and has remained one of John Duke's leading interpreters. The composer was also represented in the 1977 anthology, New World Records, with three of his Edwin Arlington Robinson songs (discussed below) as performed by Donald Gramm and Donald Hasard. In the same decade, two complete recordings of his songs were issued presenting John Duke himself at the piano: the first with Donald Boothman in 1977[28] and the second with Carole Bogard, soprano, in 1979.[29]

*   *   *

John Duke has expressed his gratitude for the advantages of an academic environment in the fostering of his creative development. One of these advantages has been the opportunity to nurture "a lively interest in philosophy and aesthetics. At one time," says Duke, "I read extensively in the philosophy of Bergson, mainly, I think, because it dealt so brilliantly with the problem of the discursive intellect when faced with the mysteries of the creative instinct. As time went on I became more and more of an anti-intellectual, especially so far as music is concerned, and more and more conscious of the limits of discursive language in trying to probe its depths."[30]

Despite these reservations, however, John Duke has continued, throughout his career, to employ his own discursive intellect and impressive verbal skills in the writing of letters and articles. He has done this in the attempt to understand and delineate his passion for vocal melody, his innately powerful response to lyric poetry, and his lifelong involvement with song, the form which combines them. In 1961, Duke explained his growing disinterest in instrumental composition in these terms:

> My early training was concentrated almost exclusively on the piano and ever since I have had a most intense interest in piano playing.... Why then have I written so little for the piano and why am I now writing exclusively for the voice?
> I think it is because of my belief that vocal utterance is at the basis of music's mystery. The thing that makes melody a concrete expression of

feeling and not just a horizontal design in tones is
its power to symbolize the pull, the tension of our
feeling of duration. In this view, all music, no
matter how complex in texture, is an extension of
our urge to sing, --to go beyond speech in intensity
and beauty of form.... I had gradually come to
feel that using words as musical material seemed
to give my songs a quality that my instrumental mu-
sic lacked. The words and their associations with
concrete situations and feelings seemed to give my
melodies a form and "authenticity" that I could not
get without them.... It may be that someday I
shall go back to writing instrumental music. But
at present I feel that the twentieth century experi-
ments in instrumental music have tended to take the
concreteness, the humanity out of melody, and I
want to be among those who are trying to bring back
this quality.[31]

Having, therefore, become committed to the use of
"words as musical material," Duke gradually developed a
technique for finding the ones he needed. He describes the
process thus:

In the course of reading literally thousands of po-
ems in English in my quest for song texts, I have
developed an ability to sense quickly, usually after
a single reading, the possibilities of a poem as mu-
sical material, at least as far as my own musical
sensibilities are concerned. What do I look for?
Lines which immediately suggest a "singable" phrase;
stanzas which offer contrast in mood and suggest
varieties of musical treatment; open vowels at cli-
mactic points; variety and subtlety in the spoken
rhythms.... But the most important thing of all
is the ability to sense the possibility.of assimilating
all of the material which the poem offers into a
strong and concise musical form.[32]

John Duke here alludes to the concept of word-setting
as "assimilation," a process in which the music swallows all
elements of the poetry to become a special (but in no way
"impure") kind of music.[33] The composer came upon the
formulation of this principle while studying the works of Su-
zanne Langer,[34] an aesthetician whose writings he describes
as "aesthetics at its best" and as "a good example of using
art to describe art."[35] In applying the assimilative principle,

Duke has been constantly "devoted to trying to realize in English the ideal of the German lied, i.e., the same intimate and inseparable relationship between the text and music."[36]

The meticulous craftsmanship which supports this philosophical concept is revealed in John Duke's description of his working methods:

> I now make a regular practice of making a "rhythmic sketch" or planning out of the time values of a melody in accordance with my feeling for the natural rhythmic utterance of the words, before I attempt to conceive the melody as definite pitch variations. Of course, this is no good if it does not become part of a really good melody but (assuming that the melody is good) it does make sure that the words will reinforce and become part of the whole melodic conception rather than seem to run counter to the melody as I think they often do in unconvincing songs.[37]

In 1981, John Duke contributed what he described as "his final word on the subject of song" to be published as the lead article in Volume I, number 1, of Ars Lyrica: the journal of the newly established Society for Word-Music Relationships. This article, entitled "The Significance of Song" and mentioned above, was characterized by Mark Van Doren, a long-time friend of the composer's, as "not a definition ... but rather a summoning of the subject, so that while one reads one hears-- ... a priceless experience."[38] What is indeed "heard" in this remarkable summation is a spiritual perspective on the meaning of song in human life. "The mystery of melody," Duke writes, "seems to reside in its creation of an experience in which time loses the character of successive moments and becomes an ever expanding present."[39] To reinforce this idea, he turned to Henri Bergson, mentor of a lifetime, and his concept of "the continuous melody of our inner life."[40] (Although she is not mentioned here, it is certainly worthy of note that Suzanne Langer makes the directly pertinent observation in her discussion of poetry that "the whole creation in a lyric is an awareness of a subjective experience, and the tense of subjectivity is the 'timeless' present."[41])

Interestingly, Duke then quotes the poem "What Are Years" by Marianne Moore, who was considered by many to be the most prosaic of poets (see Chapter I, p. 32), and whom John Duke has never set. A powerful image toward the end of the poem, however, serves him well:

> ". . . The very bird
> grown taller as he sings, steels
> his form straight up. "

From this, Duke derives that "by its very nature, song cannot be used to express a denial of life." On the contrary, he tells us, "all song . . . is saying in effect 'I am alive and I affirm the value of living.'"42

*   *   *

In a song catalog of Schubertian proportions, which is entirely based on English language poetry, John Duke has devoted fully seventy-five percent of his settings to the work of American poets. According to the composer, this does not result from a conscious exclusion, but rather from years of combing anthologies, "always thinking of the poem as I would speak it . . . and how I would transfer or transfigure the spoken word into music."43 By indirection, then, we perceive that it was the cadence of American speech and American poetry which had the most power to draw him and to suggest musical form.

Nine of the American poets represented in Duke's catalog will be discussed in this chapter and the next, and the order of their treatment will be based not on the chronology of their birth but on the historical position of the specific settings in the composer's list of works. Thus we begin with Adelaide Crapsey, born in 1878, whose "Rapunzel" was set in 1935, and conclude with Six Poems by Emily Dickinson, the earliest of the nine, who was born in 1830, but whose settings are among John Duke's most recent publications (1978).

Adelaide Crapsey (1878-1914)

Adelaide Crapsey was born in Brooklyn Heights, but her family moved to Rochester, New York, one year later, and she attended public schools there until 1893. Although her father was an Episcopalian minister, conservative thinking was hardly her heritage. Reverend Crapsey was deposed from the ministry after being tried for heresy in 1905, and her mother, Adelaide Trowbridge, of an equally unorthodox turn of mind, fostered extreme intellectual independence in each of her nine children. Despite their strength of intellect and conviction, however, the family members were marked for tragedy. Sister Ruth (age 11) died of undulant fever in 1898, sister Emily (age 24) of appendicitis in 1901, and brother Philip (age 31) of the aftereffects of malaria in 1907. Adelaide herself was doomed to end a promising academic career and artistically creative life by dying of tuberculosis at the age of thirty-six.

The poet prepared for college at Kemper Hall in Kenosha, Wisconsin, and entered Vassar in 1897. Her literary preoccupations already strengthening as an undergraduate, Crapsey became class poet and editor of the yearbook, besides appearing in several plays and belonging to the debating team. She graduated with honors and was elected to Phi Beta Kappa in 1901, then returned to Kemper Hall as a teacher of history and literature.

For the next decade, Adelaide Crapsey alternated trips to Europe for the purpose of study and travel with several teaching positions in the United States, the last and most prestigious of these being an instructorship in poetics at Smith College which she held from 1911 to 1913. Her principal area of scholarly investigation was English metrics, and she did intensive research in 1911 at the London museum for an exhaustive technical thesis entitled Analysis of English Metrics that was to remain only two-thirds completed at her death.

Although Crapsey apparently saw herself primarily as a scholar, not a poet, her study of English prosody led to a fascination with Oriental verse forms that preceded Ezra Pound's by several years. Inspired by Japanese Hokku and Tanka poetry, she created the five line "cinquain" containing fixed numbers of syllables which reduced the verbal material to its most economical terms, and wrote in this form from 1911 to 1913. By this time, an increasing physical exhaustion of ten years' duration had developed into her terminal illness, and Adelaide Crapsey spent her last months writing much of her finest poetry while knowingly awaiting death in a sanatorium at Saranac Lake, New York.

A slim volume of Crapsey's poetry appeared posthumously in 1915, entitled simply Verse. Seven poems were added to the 1922 edition, and twenty more to the one published in 1934. In these volumes are printed a few poems from 1905, the "cinquains" of 1911-1913, and the rest from 1909 on. While the earlier work treats predominantly romantic subjects in the restricted terms available to a woman of her era, the later poems become increasingly reminiscent of Emily Dickinson in their brevity, directness, obsessive preoccupation with death, and penchant for unusual punctuation (Crapsey using multiple dots in place of the Dickinson dashes).

The poem "Rapunzel" (grouped under Part II of the 1922 edition, but undated) has been given a most remarkable setting by John Duke, [44] who is strongly conscious of his Smith College faculty kinship with the ill-fated poet. He, in fact, lived just across the street from her closest friend for many years and learned a great deal about her. "Judging by her photographs," Duke writes, "she was a really beautiful woman."[45] "Rapunzel" consists of three short stanzas of four lines each. It begins in a regular iambic meter which is soon broken by the powerful thrust of the question which closes each of the three verses: "Ah, who is there?" Much of the strength of the poem comes from the dramatic immediacy of using Rapunzel herself as the speaker, as she loosens her hair and waits for the unknown. Although various interpretations of Crapsey's meaning are possible, depending on the date of the writing (which is, unfortunately, unknown) John Duke's conception of it is quite clear. "The poem," he says, "seems rather cryptic until we realize that the author was waiting for <u>death</u>, symbolized by the <u>witch</u>."[46]

The composer wrote this song in 1935 as one of a group of settings which, as previously suggested, had been influenced by his studies with Boulanger, and by his subsequent exploration of the newer compositional trends. Duke's primarily linear thinking in this period is evidenced by his suite for viola alone composed in 1933, while the songs of 1934 and 1935 are oriented toward two voice counterpoint and have a spareness of texture which places them completely apart from all the Duke settings that preceded or followed. The piano part of "Rapunzel" is actually a single line doubled at the octave and scored for two hands. Above this, the brief, punctuated vocal phrases are set in a declamatory style, in which stepwise motion is used to create a trancelike atmosphere in the narrative (see Ex. 2.1), and increasingly wide leaps to underline the speaker's mounting dread (see Ex. 2.2).

Very few Duke songs of this period carry key signatures and this one is no exception, but it would not in any case, since it opens and closes in the natural form of A minor, or the Aeolian mode. Modal elements, in fact, predominate in both vocal and instrumental lines, and they lend

Example 2.1, measures 30-37. Copyright 1947, Mercury Music, Inc.; used by permission.

Example 2.2, measures 60-68. Copyright 1947, Mercury Music, Inc.; used by permission.

an appropriate color to the retelling of the ancient fairy tale. The almost unremitting eighth-note motion is a commonly encountered rhythmic innovation in the American art song of the thirties[47] and serves the dramatic purpose of suggesting Rapunzel's restless agitation. Another and very effective twentieth-century device is the polytonal source of the final dissonance, as the singer holds an anguished high A from the tonic chord over a piano figure which mercilessly repeats the hammered suspense of the dominant (see Example 2.2).

It should be mentioned here that all verbal repetitions in this song are from the original poem. John Duke, unlike a great many song composers, has remained meticulously faithful to the text in the vast majority of his settings. On occasion, he has omitted a verse or two in order to create a more compact and manageable musical form, but even this has been rare in his catalog. Interestingly, however, the composer has, of most recent years, begun to place musical form above poetic integrity as his primary artistic goal in song writing. "If you get the form just right, it has great power,"[48] says Duke, adding that he is now more willing to change or leave out parts of poems to serve this end.

Edna St. Vincent Millay (1892-1950)

The year 1892 saw the birth of another woman poet whose childhood heritage of independent thinking was to be imprinted with the form and polish of a Vassar education. Breaking away from established patterns began for Edna Millay with the middle name chosen by her parents for their first-born child. St. Vincent's was a hospital in her home state of Maine where her sailor uncle had received excellent care after a shipwreck, and this eldest daughter of three was to be called "Vincent" by family and intimates throughout her life. Cora Buzzelle Millay, an even more strong-minded and unconventional woman than Adelaide Trowbridge Crapsey, divorced Edna's father when the girl was eight--a daring move in the year 1900. Her modest, intermittent salary as a practical nurse and frequent absences from home developed an admirable independence of spirit and indifference to material comforts in the three girls, especially Vincent as the oldest. But a far greater gift was her mother's fostering of her literary and musical talents which early began to bear fruit amid the nurturing mountains and seashore of Penobscot County, Maine.

Millay had an inborn knack for musical composition, and studied the piano quite seriously in her teens. She abandoned hopes of a concert career when her hands were pronounced too small, but for the rest of her life was to find "comfort as well as pleasure in playing and listening to music."[49] In high school, her theatrical gifts for both playwriting and acting also surfaced, but her principal vocation as poet became clearly established with the acceptance, in 1912, of "Renascence" by an American poetical anthology called The Lyric Year. The enormous outcry over her poem having failed to win a prize brought her instant literary notoriety, as well as the attention of Caroline P. Dow who arranged funding so that she might enroll in Vassar College for the academic training which her talent and intellect warranted.

A semester of pre-Vassar preparation at Barnard College in the spring of 1913 enabled Millay to sample the artistic climate of New York City at the moment in time when modern poetry was just beginning to challenge traditional forms on the American scene. (An analogous development in the world of visual art was the legendary "armory show," --the International Art Exhibit which the young woman attended in March.) The literary world was eager to meet her, and during a memorable party hosted by Jessie Rittenhouse, then secretary to the Poetry Society of America, the poet was introduced to some of its leading figures, including Sara Teasdale and Witter Bynner. The latter had written an admiring note to Millay concerning "Renascence" at the time of its publication, together with another poet, Arthur Davison Ficke, who would become one of the most beloved persons in her life.

The rules and regulations of Vassar proved trying to the poet's nature, but its literary offerings nourished her mind, and its strong interests in drama and singing gave her further creative outlets. In 1917, her senior year, Millay responded to Sara Teasdale's request to reprint her poem, "Ashes of Life," in The Answering Voice, Teasdale's anthology of love poetry by women. In a sprightly letter, the young poet teased the experienced one, only a few years married to Ernst Filsinger, saying "Whadda you mean having husbands and anthologies at the same time?"[50] One wonders if this flippant reference to a marriage already going sour, coupled with Teasdale's distrust of Millay's unconventional approach to life may have been among the factors which militated against the growth of a friendship between them. It is nevertheless true that just before her suicide in 1933, Sara Teasdale wrote to Edna Millay of her early admiration, which had apparently survived the passage of the years. "I like to think," she said, "that when I first read you long ago, I knew you and named a star."51

Following graduation came the famous Greenwich Village years which saw Millay's association with the Provincetown Players as actress, playwright, and director, and publications in Vanity Fair, The Dial, Harriet Monroe's Poetry and the Mirror, a St. Louis journal edited by W. M. Reedy. Her poetry collection, A Few Figs from Thistles, appeared in 1920, and the couplet beginning "My candle burns at both ends" was seized upon, somewhat to the poet's later dismay, as the motto of a generation eager to throw off the shackles of Victorian propriety. The Edna St. Vincent Millay of this period possessed a compelling beauty and personality which drew her into relationships with a number of men of her literary circle. Among them were the playwright Floyd Dell, Edmund Wilson, and Witter Bynner, all of whom unsuccessfully proposed marriage. Ironically, Arthur Davison Ficke, whom she loved deeply all her life after their meeting and affair in 1918, did not ask her to be his wife, even when his first marriage dissolved.

The poems of Second April, published in 1921, include a number of sonnets written in the lonely aftermath of the Ficke encounter. The sonnet was to become one of her most characteristic and successful forms as she poured the new wine of contemporary speech into the old bottles of the prescribed metric and rhyme schemes. Returning home in ill health from a European writing stint for Vanity Fair, Millay was married in 1923 to Eugen Boissevain, a businessman with a deep admiration for the arts. He was twelve years older than the poet and this fact, coupled with his devotion to her talent, gave her the sense of the fatherly care she had never experienced, as well as the assurance that she would not have to bury her Muse in domesticity. The decade of the twenties also saw the development of a strong friendship with Elinor Wylie whose Nets to Catch the Wind had been given a glowing review by Millay in the New York Evening Post of January, 1922. When the League of American Penwomen snubbed Wylie because of her personal life, Edna Millay refused their proffered honors in a scathing letter, and she poured her grief over the tragic early death of Elinor Wylie into a number of poems which were published in Huntsman What Quarry? (1939).

By 1935, Millay had reached the peak of her career, with her writing much in demand and requests increasing for her highly dramatic readings of her own poetry. A strong social conscience which had involved her in the Sacco-Vanzetti case and the post-World War I pacifist movement, now impelled her toward the Spanish Loyalist cause, and a heavy investment of time and effort in propaganda for the Allied effort in World War II. Increasing physical problems caused a breakdown when the war ended, and she was just beginning to respond to her husband's dedicated care when he died following surgery in 1949. After a single year of reclusive, grief-stricken life, the poet had a heart-attack on the stairs at "Steepletop, " their home in the Berkshires since 1925, and joined him in death.

The twelve love-sonnets of Millay's Second April are followed by an eight line poem called "Wild Swans" which concludes the volume. Its brevity and irregular lines sprinkled with bold metric choices are in direct contrast to the preceding sonnets, as is the force of its compressed emotion. In it, Millay, who all her life had a passionate attachment to wild birds and natural beauty, finds release in the flight of the swans from her "tiresome heart, forever living and dying. " She leaves her "house without air" and exhorts the swans to fly "over the town again" with a cry that seems to celebrate their unsullied freedom while it carries an echo of human pain.

John Duke chose this poem for setting in 1935, [52] the same year as "Rapunzel, " but in this song, contours of the severe linear approach have been somewhat softened as chordal elements return and the piano has two hands independently occupied. Duke now begins to exhibit a style which is typical of many of his finest songs. In a process very close to that of instrumental chamber music, voice and piano each carry their own motivic material, the two lines for the most part unrelated, yet indissolubly meshed. Thus, we find the accompaniment motif expressed in the piano prelude:

Example 2.3, measures 1-4. Copyright 1947, Mercury Music, Inc. ; used by permission.

61

and reentering around the vocal line at another pitch level.

Example 2.4, measures 29-32. Copyright 1947, Mercury Music, Inc.; used by permission.

A possible connection between the two emerges near the end of the song as the voice picks up the large interval leaps from the piano motif.

Example 2.5, measures 50-53. Copyright 1947, Mercury Music, Inc.; used by permission.

These large intervals which are for the most part intensified by leaping from a short note to a longer one, create an aural context of desperate "abandon," the quality called for in the composer's marking (see Example 2.3). The longing implicit in the poem is perfectly translated by John Duke into suspended dissonances such as the first right hand piano note of measures one and two respectively, and the vocal pitches of E natural and E flat in Example 2.5. The char-

acteristic leaps and suspensions receive their final statement
in the piano postlude which loses energy in the diminishing
dynamic level but retains much unresolved emotion in the ex-
tended minor ninth that ends the song.

The fluid metric scheme of continuous eighth-note mo-
tion with varying numbers of beats per measure is carried
on here from "Rapunzel," and becomes a perfect foil for the
unpredictable poetic feet of Millay's poem.   A key signature
is still absent, but tonal areas are clear, with D minor the
principal key.   Two interesting chromatic modulations are
dictated by the text, both moving upward tonally to parallel
images of flight.   The first begins as follows and ends with
Example 2.4,

Example 2.6, measures 25-28.   Copyright 1947, Mercury
Music, Inc.; used by permission.

and the second has been cited above as Example 2.5.

Edwin Arlington Robinson (1869-1935)

E. A. Robinson's life, one totally devoted to the writing of
poetry, was almost equally divided between the nineteenth and
twentieth centuries, and he is generally recognized as the
most important poet writing in America in the year 1900.
He had grown up in Gardiner, Maine, as the virtually ig-
nored youngest son of Edward and Mary Palmer Robinson
who had desperately wanted their third child to be a daugh-
ter.   Most of the parental attention, therefore, turned to

Dean, the intellectual, who became a physician and eventually a drug addict, and to Herman, the handsome extrovert, who ruined the family business and sought refuge in alcohol. Edwin entered Harvard in 1891, but had to leave a year later when his father died, a death that was followed with tragic haste by his mother's in 1896 and brother Dean's in 1899.

Having no recourse to family support after his mother died and with his work as yet unrecognized, the poet was forced to hold a number of non-literary jobs for short periods of time. These varied from administrative assistant to Harvard's President Eliot, to time-checker for the construction of the first New York subway. His reluctance to continue to do anything that took him from his writing and his scorn for the prevailing materialism of society was evidenced in a letter of this period to Harry deForest Smith "... This diabolical, dirty race that men are running after (dollars) disgusts me.... Business be damned," said Robinson.[53]

In 1905, Theodore Roosevelt was so impressed by a reading of his poetry collection Children of the Night that he wrote a critical review of it in The Outlook and had Robinson appointed to a position in the New York Collector of Customs' office which he held until 1909. In that year, brother Herman died and Robinson returned to Gardiner in the hope of reestablishing a relationship with Herman's widow, Emma Shepherd Robinson, whom he had loved since high school. This failing, he devoted the rest of his life to producing a prodigious number of volumes of poetry which at last began to bring him fame and a modest living.

By 1913, Robinson was publishing in Harper's and the Atlantic Monthly; in 1921 he received the first of three Pulitzer Prizes to be given him in six years' time; and in 1922 he was awarded honorary doctorates by Yale University and Bowdoin College. The last twenty-four summers of his life were spent at the MacDowell Colony in Peterborough, New Hampshire (see Chapter I, p. 9-10) and there are many accounts of meetings with him there during those years. Mary Colum relates an exchange in the dining room of the Colony when the poet, with his "dry Yankee humor," told Harriet Monroe of Poetry magazine that he was unable to work, and was having to take a course in poetry from Colum to awaken his mind.[54] John Duke also remembers meeting Robinson during a visit to the Colony and shaking hands with him. "He was," says the composer, "MacDowell's 'prize catch'--a strange, withdrawn creature, but in my opinion, one of our greatest poets."[55]

Robinson's historical position as a straddler of two centuries and their prevailing systems of thought, accounts for the major sources of tension which fed his poetic gift. Torn all his life between Emersonian Idealism and the newer scientific philosophy of Naturalism, he shared also in the dilemma of those poets who rejected the free verse structures of the modern poetry movement but incorporated a new freedom of content in their work. "The Imagists," he told Amy Lowell, "seem to me rather too self-conscious and exclusive to stand the test of time" but added "I don't care a pinfeather what form a poem is written in so long as it makes me sit up."56

What did not make Robinson sit up were the celebrations of nature that had been the preoccupation of his Romantic forbears. He turned instead in his own poetry to an emphasis on people with the avowed purpose of showing "that men and women are individuals."57 His particular combination of compassion and irony became a legacy for many of the twentieth-century poets who followed, as did his willingness to introduce comic elements into serious poetry.58 One characteristic that Robinson shared with many of his fellow poets, past and future, was a responsiveness to music that had begun in Gardiner with a limited study of both violin and clarinet. In time he came to feel that music and poetry were closely allied as forms of artistic expression, "music being poetry and poetry being music," as he wrote to a friend.59

Robinson's prolific output includes more narrative than lyrical poetry, and all of it demonstrates an impressive variety of verse forms. His reputation today is based largely on his early work, the short character sketches of people who live in a place called Tilbury Town. This city is generally accepted to be a poetic representation of Gardiner, Maine, and the eccentric misfits and failures of Robinson's portraits to derive, at least in part, from the poet's view of himself and his brothers. In 1945, John Duke set three of these short narratives:60 "Richard Cory" and "Luke Havergal" from Children of the Night (1897) and "Miniver Cheevy" from The Town Down the River (1910). Written ten years after "Rapunzel" and "Wild Swans" (with only half a dozen songs between), these three, in accordance with the totally different needs of the Robinson texts, exhibit a broad, dynamic, vigorous style with an expansive "pianism" that Duke is employing for the first time.

The sixteen lines of the poem "Richard Cory" present a well-drawn sketch of a rich and elegant man who "glittered when he walked" as perceived by his envious fellows. In a surprise ending involving only the final couplet, Richard Cory goes home "one calm summer night" to "put a bullet through his head." It has been suggested that Cory is a thinly disguised Herman Robinson, whose personal qualities showed such promise, but who destroyed himself slowly with alcohol after his disastrous investments of 1893. Herman did not actually die until 1909, twelve years after the publication of Children of the Night, but the contrast between his charming exterior and inward despair may well have been apparent to his brother during the period when those poems were being written (1890-1897).

Duke's rhythmic scheme in the setting of "Richard Cory" is one of its most interesting aspects, as he translates the unwavering iambic pentameter of the text into not one but two different metric patterns. While the lilting, sophisticated 6/8 accompaniment figures present Cory's musical portrait, the voice of the narrator sings in the blunt, square 2/4 of the less privileged townspeople.

Example 2.7, measures 17-20. Copyright 1948, Carl Fischer, Inc.; used by permission.

The steady, pianistic motion of six eighth notes to the bar comes to seem like the very thread of the protagonist's life and indeed it stops only in the measure in which the bullet ends it (see Ex. 2.8).

In the songs of the forties, John Duke returns to notated key signatures, and "Richard Cory" has three tonal areas: a lightly scored B flat major opening which sets the stage, a modulating bridge passage between verses three and four which moves through A major, and a third section in D

66

Example 2.8, measures 89-93. Copyright 1948, Carl Fischer, Inc.; used by permission.

flat major. This final key has a more heavily scored piano part, whose pitch and dynamic levels rise with the growing envy of the townfolk.

Example 2.9, measures 69-73. Copyright 1948, Carl Fischer, Inc.; used by permission.

Musical word-painting is also an effective device in this setting, as a tremulous accompaniment figure suggests "fluttering pulses" (see Ex. 2.10) and multiple grace notes at brilliant pitch levels approach an aural equivalent of "glitter" (see Ex. 2.11).

Robinson's obsessive feelings for the beautiful Emma Shepherd, who became his sister-in-law, gave rise to many poems about love unfulfilled or lost forever. "Luke Havergal," characterized by the poet as his "uncomfortable abstraction,"[61] is one of the most haunting of these, despite a cer-

67

Example 2.10, measures 46-48. Copyright 1948, Carl Fischer, Inc.; used by permission.

Example 2.11, measures 49-53. Copyright 1948, Carl Fischer, Inc.; used by permission.

tain ambiguity which led Theodore Roosevelt to write that he liked the poem, but was not sure he understood it. In these verses, Luke Havergal, apparently mourning a dead love, is never described but is rather addressed, in a monologue by a ghostly messenger "out of a grave" who points to "the western gate" as "the one way to where she is." This theme of lovers being reunited in death provided the occasion for Duke's composition of one of his finest Romantic ballads which offers a gratifying vehicle to singer and pianist at the same time that it captures the brooding passion of the text.

Robinson's "Luke Havergal" has four verses, but this is one of the rare instances mentioned above in which John Duke omits part of the poem in his setting. In a tight, workable ABA structure, he sets the first and last stanzas which deal with the "western gate"[62] in the key of E flat major, and creates an eerie G sharp minor contrasting section for the third verse in which the messenger describes his other-worldly origins.

Example 2.12a, measures 9-12. Copyright 1948, Carl Fischer, Inc.; used by permission.

Example 2.12b, measures 85-88. Copyright 1948, Carl Fischer, Inc.; used by permission.

Example 2.12c, measures 47-50. Copyright 1948, Carl Fischer, Inc.; used by permission.

This three-part form necessitates the omission of stanza two, and one line of the fourth stanza is also omitted to impel the musical/dramatic climax. In all other ways Duke remains faithful to the text, including the verbal repetitions which close each verse.

Example 2.13, measures 37-41. Copyright 1948, Carl Fischer, Inc.; used by permission.

John Duke's writing for the piano in "Luke Havergal" begins to exhibit the neo-Romantic idiom in the figurations which is typical of this period. Passages in parallel thirds and octaves, and widely spread broken chord patterns build an enveloping world of sound around Havergal's mystical ecstacy (see Example 2.12b). The melodic contour of the entire song is one of Duke's most lyrical inventions, and takes on quasi-operatic dimensions in the climactic line which rises an octave and a fourth in a shattering crescendo.

Example 2.14, measures 104-106. Copyright 1948, Carl Fischer, Inc.; used by permission.

One of the strongest portraits among the citizens of Tilbury Town is "Miniver Cheevy" who has been aptly termed the "archetypal frustrated romantic idealist."[63] It is easy to credit a not uncommon opinion among literary critics that Miniver, a "child of scorn" who "had reasons" to regret "that he was ever born" is Robinson himself: an unwanted son to whom life had brought considerably more pain than happiness. The poet too, like Miniver, had been drawn to the glories of past ages, had mourned the low status of "Romance" and "Art" in the present, and had "scorned the gold he sought" in a life-long conflict between the struggle to live decently and a revulsion toward the materialism of society. In the last two stanzas of eight, Miniver is revealed as a dreamer lost in thought and the consolations of alcohol, but the prevailing tone of the poem is ironic rather than tragic, and the writer's compassion for his anti-hero is evident.

John Duke's setting of "Miniver Cheevy" is an admirably crafted set of variations based on a theme which both outlines the contours of the vocal line, and establishes the harmonic background in passacaglia style.

Example 2.15, measures 1-8. Copyright 1948, Carl Fischer, Inc.; used by permission.

The nine variations which follow account for the eight verses of the poem plus an epilogue, and in them the composer employs all the traditional musical devices of variation in the service of the text. "The days of old ... when steeds were prancing" is set with an accompaniment figure whose meter and rhythmic pattern is clearly suggestive of horses' hooves.

Example 2.16, measures 17-20. Copyright 1948, Carl Fischer, Inc.; used by permission.

The third and fourth verses in which Miniver sighs for past glories and mourns over the prosaic present call for slow tempi and the "dolorous" key of G minor. In contrast, verse five portrays his identification with the nobility of the Medici in terms of G major, a faster tempo and a majestic piano figure which covers the keyboard in broad, sweeping gestures.

Example 2.17, measures 41-42. Copyright 1948, Carl Fischer, Inc.; used by permission.

As evidenced from the last two examples, John Duke has preceded the tempo marking of each variation with an adjective that indicates the mood to be established by the performers. For variation VIII he chooses "tipsy," and the piano writing now takes on a lurching quality, which culminates in the rapidly descending arpeggio of measure 72, suggestive of a drunken fall.

Example 2.18, measures 69-72. Copyright 1948, Carl Fischer, Inc.; used by permission.

Example 2.19, measures 73-83. Copyright 1948, Carl Fischer, Inc.; used by permission.

73

The musical humor is deftly amplified in the epilogue, with
minimal textual additions by the composer which are rare for
Duke. Miniver, now obviously intoxicated, tries to imitate
the piano's melodic fragments in canonic style. He begins
boldly on "ah," but his imitations become softer and more
grunt-like, then fail to find the correct pitch, and eventually
trail off into merciful oblivion (see Ex. 2.19).

Elinor Wylie (1885-1928)

The life of Elinor Wylie has been discussed at some length
in Chapter I along with Mary Howe's settings of her poetry.
John Duke had met this writer "in the late twenties, just be-
fore she died, at an evening of poetry and music in the home
of Grace Hazard Conkling, professor of English at Smith and
a poet herself. Elinor read one of her longer poems" con-
tinues Duke. "She was rather gaunt and ill-looking at the
time, having lost most of her extraordinary beauty. It was
not until some years after that I began to set her poems."[64]
John Duke's first Wylie setting, written in 1946, was "Bells
in the Rain."[65] It met with almost instant success, being
performed just two years later by Povla Frisch in a New
York recital.[66] The poem bearing the same title appeared
in Nets to Catch the Wind, the volume which in 1921 estab-
lished the previously unknown writer as a major talent on the
American literary scene. In this collection, Wylie issued
Athena-like from Zeus' forehead, as it were, with fully de-
veloped control over her "craftsman's concern for phrasing,
and for the sensuous qualities of words."[67]

"Bells in the Rain" again demonstrates the Wylie pre-
dilection for compression, and consists of three four-line
stanzas of iambic tetrameter punctuated by an occasional
dactyl. In it, the "limpid drops of rain" falling on the town
bring peaceful sleep which is "unheeded [by] the dead" but
welcomed "most tenderly" by the living. Sensuous, indeed,
in verbal components and visual images is the opening of
verse two: "the bright drops ring like bells of glass,"--and
it is this phrase which provides John Duke with the most im-
portant musical element of his setting. Beginning in the in-
troduction and continuing throughout the song there is a pi-
anistic figure of quietly insistent sixteenth notes placed high
on the keyboard. The brilliant overtones of the pitches cre-

ate a cross-sensory suggestion of glass, while the many intervals of fourths and fifths take on the melodic configurations of bells.

Example 2.20, measures 1-4. Copyright 1948, Carl Fischer, Inc.; used by permission.

Against this steady accompaniment of the bell-like rain drops, the vocal line is principally structured to suggest the peaceful descent of sleep. Sharing in this musical effect are the falling pitch levels and sustained length of "sleep falls" and the pianissimo dynamic level which dominates most of the song.

Example 2.21, measures 9-10. Copyright 1948, Carl Fischer, Inc.; used by permission.

Harmonic contexts involving both voice and piano combine in two of the most telling moments of the setting. For "The bright drops ring like bells of glass," Duke moves from his E minor tonality through the subdominant to an altered chord on the sub-mediant. The resulting brightness of the C sharp major touch lends the required brilliance in a device that is very reminiscent of Griffes' procedures in "Evening Song" discussed in Volume I of this series. [68]

Example 2.22, measures 15-18. Copyright 1948, Carl Fischer, Inc.; used by permission.

In the final line of the song, the pivotal word "tenderly" is highlighted not only by its subito pianissimo following a surprising octave leap, but also by the change in its chordal meaning from root position in a G major triad, to a softer and more ambiguous situation as the seventh of the subdominant (see Ex. 2.23).

"Little Elegy" had already been set by Mary Howe in 1934 (see Chapter I, p. 11), and it is extremely interesting to compare hers with Duke's equally successful but quite different treatment composed twelve years later. [69] Both are in minor keys, considered appropriate by both composers for this

Example 2.23, measures 33-37. Copyright 1948, Carl Fischer, Inc.; used by permission.

tribute to a lost love.[70] Both are lyrical settings, with carefully molded and effective vocal contours. Howe's setting, however, puts much more emphasis on the piano with a more elaborate accompaniment throughout whereas Duke's piano writing is quiet and chordal, with some motivic imitation of the voice. Each gives particular harmonic attention to the line "If never seen your sweetest face" and Duke travels all the way from his one flat tonic (D minor) to the six sharps of F sharp major.

Example 2.24, measures 11-16. Copyright © 1949, G. Schirmer, Inc.; used by permission.

For the climactic lines "No bird have grace / Or pow'r to sing / Or anything / Be kind or fair," Howe chooses to let the piano complete the emotional expression with two more measures of pianistic crescendo. John Duke, however, has it happen primarily in the vocal line, with several leaps to high sustained pitches while accompanied by unobtrusive rising chordal sequences.

Example 2.25, measures 17-26. Copyright © 1949, G. Schirmer, Inc.; used by permission.

Finally, it should be noted that Mary Howe's setting repeats the final phrase "And you / Nowhere," while John Duke's, in characteristic faithfulness to the original text, does not.

"The Bird" was printed in Wylie's posthumous Collected Poems of 1932 as one of those grouped in the "Hitherto Uncollected" section. Of these poems, some had previously appeared in periodicals and others had never been published. In the first of these two contrasting short stanzas the bird is exhorted to "sing again" by the poet who is listening to the rain fall "through the long night." In the second, the bird has returned, and his "clearest voice" makes the "rain sing / And the dark rejoice." John Duke had his setting of this poem printed together with "Little Elegy," and "The Bird,"[71] which was dedicated to the Brazilian soprano Bidu Sayao, is one of his most frequently performed songs.

The chordal nature of the accompaniment seems to relate to "Little Elegy" but this is a much more passionate statement, as Duke uses the poetic repetition to build crescendos of pitch and dynamics.

Example 2.26, measures 5-8. Copyright © 1949, G. Schirmer, Inc.; used by permission.

A new element entering the accompaniment is the pianistic imitation of bird-song which the composer effectively employs in the formal structure as prelude, interlude between the two verses, and postlude.

Example 2.27, measures 1-4. Copyright © 1949, G. Schirmer, Inc.; used by permission.

Key change is the device which most clearly embodies

79

the contrast between the stanzas. The opening in B minor suggests the poet's longing for the absent singer (see Examples 2.26 and 2.27). A turn to F major after the interlude brings with it a surge of hope

Example 2.28, measures 18-22. Copyright © 1949, G. Schirmer, Inc.; used by permission.

and leads to the triumphant establishment of D major which holds through the quietly joyful conclusion.

Example 2.29, measures 27-30. Copyright © 1949, G. Schirmer, Inc.; used by permission.

Also among the "Hitherto Uncollected" poems of 1932, but far different in mood and statement, is "Viennese Waltz." This poem is characteristic of the many in which Wylie expressed a sense of impending disaster: not surprising in an artist whose life had encompassed divorce, social ostracism, miscarriage, the suicide of relatives, and a constant struggle against the pain of chronic illness. In "Viennese Waltz," the speaker addresses a partner whose "face is like a mournful pearl" in the hopes that the dancing will assuage their sadness and enable a momentary escape from "the tiger-snarling" in the night.

John Duke's setting of "Viennese Waltz"[72] which he composed in 1948 is conceived on a grand scale with a dramatic vocal line and demanding piano part. The original metric scheme of the four-verse poem has five accents per line, but this has been completely swallowed by Duke's 3/4 time. This transformation he achieves quite convincingly through a lengthening of certain vocal syllables and the imposition of a pianistic waltz background.

Example 2.30, measures 7-18. Copyright 1950, R. D. Row Music Co.; used by permission.

Throughout the song, the voice moves in fairly broad patterns of quarter and half notes suggesting the helplessness of the doomed couple (see Example 2.30) while the accompaniment soon begins to break up into eighth notes and triplets as the gyrations of the dancing become more frenetic.

81

Example 2.30 also illustrates the composer's skillful use of delayed resolution of dissonance, as the tied-over A flat on the word "tired" establishes the mood of disillusioned but yearning desire for peace and happiness which pervades the song. The chromaticism of the piano's introductory sequences is continued in all the instrumental interludes which are appropriately more reminiscent of the brooding brilliance of Chopin than of Johann Strauss' mindless Vienna.

Example 2.31, measures 37-47. Copyright 1950, R. D. Row Music Co.; used by permission.

In the last two lines of the poem, the dancers seem to be choosing to confront their doom in a dream-like state that will mitigate its harshness:

> "Come, let us dream the little death that hovers
> Pensive as heaven in a cloudy veil."

John Duke's musical clothing of this verbal withdrawal of energy takes the form of soft, sustained, high-pitched vocal sounds over equally quiet, "cloudy" altered chords which eventually retard to motionlessness. The dancers' world has ended: "not with a bang but a whimper."

Example 2.32, measures 166-182. Copyright 1950, R. D. Row Music Co.; used by permission.

NOTES

1. The American baritone, John Seagle, in an interview with the author at his home, San Antonio, Texas, May 17, 1982.

2. The Seagle colony was started in 1916 by Oscar Seagle (John Seagle's father) who was also a leading American baritone and teacher. The colony, founded on a 100-acre tract of land on Schroon Lake in upper New York State, trains young singers in vocal technique and performance.

3. Virgil Thomson, "The American Song, " The Art of Judging Music (New York: Knopf, 1948).

4. Virgil Thomson, "The Concert Song, " ibid., p. 88.

5. In a letter to the author, dated September 1, 1978, John Duke indicated his willingness to make copies of his unpublished songs available at cost (printing and mailing). Concerning his out-of-print songs, he commented "... I have the assurance of the Directors of Publication at Schirmer, Fischer, and Boosey and Hawkes, that an order for any of my 'out-of-print' songs addressed directly to them will procure a copy at a cost of 50 cents a page...." At this writing, plans are underway for a new edition of Duke's out-of-print songs, as well as for publication of those still in manuscript. Date is uncertain.

6. A to-date catalog in the NATS Bulletin, volume XXXVI: 1 (Sept/Oct 1979), lists 209 of John Duke's songs, together with text source, publication status, and date of composition.

7. Letter to the author, dated July 5, 1981.

8. The author's visit in John Duke's home, July 28-30, 1982, produced impressions of an unpretentious but inviting setting for an artist. The furnishings of a large downstairs living room include a Chinese rug, Breughel print, and a grand piano piled high with publications and manuscripts. One of the upstairs bedrooms has become a study and contains an upright piano, books on many subjects, and a collection of photographs, scrapbooks, and mementos.

9. Letter to the author, dated June 13, 1982. The majority of the biographical data on John Duke was provided the author by the composer. Information on the Seagle Colony was drawn from the Seagle interview (see note 1) and the author's visit to the colony (July 30-August 2, 1982).

10. In 1969, John Duke received the Peabody Alumni Association Award for distinguished service to music.

11. Gustav Klemm, "Gustav Strube: The Man and the Musician, " Musical Quarterly, XXVIII (July, 1942), pp. 288-301.

12. See Chapter I, p. 8.

13. Ibid. The Duke quotation is from a letter to the author dated December 19, 1981.

14. John and Dorothy Duke had a son, who lives and works in New York, and a daughter, Karen, who has carried on the musical traditions of the family. Like her paternal grandmother, Karen sings and plays the guitar as does her daughter, Morgan, and the two have frequently performed together.

15. For many years, while living in Northampton, Dorothy Duke wrote a poetry column for an area newspaper.

16. Dorothy Duke wrote the book and lyrics for John Duke's musical shows The Yankee Pedlar and The Cat That Walked By Himself. She also served as his opera librettist on the occasions indicated in the text.

17. All three of these compositions are out of print.

18. John Duke was introduced to the Seagle Colony through his daughter, Karen, who was enrolled there as a voice student for several summers in the early fifties. Also, John Seagle had come to know Duke's songs through his coach-accompanist, Nathan Price, and had performed a group of them at a New York recital in 1952.

19. The fact of Duke's birthday having belatedly come to light, it was celebrated on August 1st. Helen Seagle, John's efficient and hospitable wife, arranged birthday cake and ice cream for the entire school following dinner in "the white house," as the colony's central structure is called.

20. In a conversation with the author on July 28, 1982, Duke recalled the atmosphere at the Yaddo estate as an uncomfortable one, created by enormous and newly acquired wealth. One bedroom, he recalled, was larger than his present generously proportioned living room.

21. In regard to this première, Duke mentioned in a conversation with the author on August 2, 1982, that Sessions wrote very slowly and only had the first two movements of the sonata completed for the occasion. "Later," Duke said, "I played the whole thing at Smith, and then again in New York."

22. John Seagle, in the May, 1982 interview, described a colorful Gottschalk evening which occurred during Duke's sabbatical year at Trinity University. In connection with a series of fund-raising dinners called "Texas Under Six Flags," John Duke was persuaded to impersonate the nineteenth-century composer in old fashioned evening clothes and cape, under the

supposition that the Louisiana-born Gottschalk might well have concertized in the Republic of Texas.

23. Letter from John Duke to the author, dated June 18, 1961.

24. John Duke, "Some Reflections on the Art Song in English," The American Music Teacher, XXV: 4 (1976), p. 26.

25. John Duke, "The Significance of Song," Ars Lyrica, I (1981), pp. 11-21.

26. Participants in this panel discussion were John Duke, British composer Iain Hamilton who was at that time Mary Duke Biddle Professor of Music, and Professor Bernard Duffey, an American poetry scholar from Duke University's Department of English. The singers who performed with Duke in the recital of his songs were Claudia Bray, soprano; John Hanks, tenor (Duke University professor of voice); and Richard Rivers, bass-baritone (professor of voice at Converse College).

27. John K. Hanks and Ruth C. Friedberg, Art Song in America, vols. I and II (Durham, North Carolina: Duke University Press, 1966 and 1974). The writer appears in these recordings as accompanist and author of jacket notes.

28. Donald Boothman and John Duke, Seventeen Songs by John Duke (Washington, D.C.: Golden Age Recordings, 1977).

29. Carole Bogard and John Duke, Songs by John Duke (Framingham, Mass.: Cambridge Records, 1979).

30. The foregoing paragraph and quotations are drawn from a letter dated September 2, 1979, to Louis Auld, editor of the periodical Ars Lyrica and a former colleague of John Duke's on the Smith College faculty. The reader should be advised that the underlining in this and all Duke quotations is the composer's.

31. Letter to the author, dated June 18, 1961.

32. Duke, "Some Reflections on the Art Song in English." In a letter to the author dated December 29, 1980, John Duke commented "as a corollary to this, I have rejected thousands of poems because I have found them, either as a whole or in part, unassimilable."

33. See American Art Song and American Poetry, vol. I, p. 16.

34. Susanne K. Langer, Feeling and Form (New York: Scribner's, 1953), chapter 10. The reader is also referred to two other works by Langer which contain illuminating treatments of both poetry and song: Philosophy in a New Key (Cambridge: Harvard University Press, 1951); and Problems of Art (New York: Charles Scribner's Sons, 1957).

35. Auld letter. One might speculate as to whether Langer's "artistic" approach to the arts was related to the fact that she herself was an amateur cellist of some accomplishment. Professor Gerard Jaffe of Incarnate Word College in San Antonio, Texas, recalls playing string quartets with her ca. 1960 when he was on the music faculty of Wesleyan University and Langer taught at the nearby Connecticut College for Women. He remembers her as a strong personality and an enthusiastic player who had a fondness for the literature which afforded notable cello solos.

36. Duke, "Some Reflections on the Art Song in English."

37. Letter of June 18, 1961 to the author.

38. Letter from Mark Van Doren to John Duke, February 11, 1971.

39. Duke, "The Significance of Song," p. 14.

40. Ibid.

41. Langer, Feeling and Form, p. 268.

42. Duke, "The Significance of Song," p. 17.

43. Conversation with the author, July 29, 1982.

44. John Duke, "Rapunzel" (New York: Mercury Music, 1947). Soprano. Range: e^1 to a^2.

45. Letter to the author, dated October 22, 1981.

46. Ibid.

47. William Treat Upton, Supplement to Art Song in America (Philadelphia: Oliver Ditson, 1938).

48. Conversation with the author, July 31, 1982. In discussing the importance of form, Duke also expressed his belief that "a song must end, not just stop. One must feel that everything has been said that needs to be."

49. Jean Gould, The Poet and Her Book (New York: Dodd, Mead, 1969), p. 49.

50. Norman A. Brittin, Edna St. Vincent Millay (New York: Twayne, 1967), p. 31.

51. Gould, p. 46.

52. John Duke, "Wild Swans" (New York: Mercury Music, 1947). Medium voice. Range: d1 to a2. Out of print. Held by Duke University music library.

53. Hoyt C. Franchere, Edwin Arlington Robinson (New York: Twayne, 1968), p. 22.

54. Colum, pp. 374-376.

55. Letter to the author, dated October 22, 1981.

56. Franchere, p. 25.

57. W. R. Robinson, Edwin Arlington Robinson: A Poetry of the Act (Cleveland: The Press of Western Reserve University, 1967), p. 51.

58. Nancy Joyner, "Edwin Arlington Robinson," Great Writers of the English Language--Poetry, ed. James Vinson (New York: St. Martin's, 1979), p. 826.

59. Letter to Arthur Nevin, quoted in Franchere, p. 29.

60. John Duke, "Richard Cory" (New York: Carl Fischer, 1948). Baritone. Range: a to e2. John Duke, "Luke Havergal" (New York: Carl Fischer, 1948). Baritone. Range: b to f2. John Duke, "Miniver Cheevy" (New York: Carl Fischer, 1948). Baritone. Range: g to f2. All three of these songs are performed by Donald Gramm and Donald Hasard on the recording called But Yesterday Is Not Today, issued in 1977 by New World Records and mentioned above in the text.

61. Franchere, p. 103.

62. An alternate interpretation to "the western gate" as a symbol for death was suggested to the author by William Walker, a leading Metropolitan Opera baritone for the past several decades. In his view, "the western gate" was the overseas passage from England to the New World, which Luke Havergal had to undertake to find his beloved, already departed on that journey.

63. Hyatt H. Waggoner, American Poets from the Puritans to the Present (New York: Dell, 1968), p. 282.

64. Letter to the author, October 22, 1981.

65. John Duke, "Bells in the Rain" (New York: Carl Fischer, 1948). High voice. Range e^1 to g^2.

66. See p. 45.

67. Babette Deutsch, Poetry in Our Time (Garden City, New York: Doubleday, 1963), p. 252.

68. See American Art Song and American Poetry, vol. I, p. 34.

69. John Duke, "Little Elegy" and "The Bird" (New York: G. Schirmer, 1949). Soprano. Range: f^1 to a^2. Out of print. Available from T.I.S. Music Shoppe, P.O. Box 1998, Bloomington, IN 47401. Also held by Duke University music library.

70. Stanley Olson in his biography called Elinor Wylie, a Life Apart (New York: Dial, 1947) treats the poet's final passion for Henry Clifford Woodhouse as largely a creation of her imagination. Little evidence, in truth, is extant in regard to the exact nature of the relationship.

71. See note 69.

72. John Duke, "Viennese Waltz" (Boston: R. D. Row Music, 1950). Selling agent: Carl Fischer. Medium high voice. Range c^1 to a flat^2. May be out of print. Available from T.I.S. Music Shoppe (see note 69) and held by Duke University music library.

III. John Duke 2.

Sara Teasdale (1884-1933), Robert Frost (1874-1963),
e.e. cummings* (1894-1962), Mark Van Doren (1894-
1972), Emily Dickinson (1830-1886).

Teasdale and Elinor Wylie were born just one year apart and
their formative years were similar in one important respect.
Each had a dominant, controlling mother, who by example and
conviction upheld the ideal of a narrowly conventional life for
women. Sara Teasdale's birthplace was St. Louis, which in
the 1880's was a large, commercial city of vigorous culture
but an atmosphere of increasing conservatism. [1] She was the
child of aging parents (born sixteen years after her nearest
sibling), and soon demonstrated a proclivity toward ill health
which resulted in part from their over-anxious attention. Her
father, a gentle, prosperous businessman, was descended
from a dissenting Baptist who had left England in 1792 for
New Jersey. Her mother traced her American ancestors
back to Captain Simon Willard, who helped to found Concord,
Massachusetts, in 1635. Sara felt a strong connection to this
Puritan heritage, although her maternal grandmother had
turned away from it, and like the Teasdales, had become a
Baptist.

John Warren Teasdale provided his family with an ele-
gant upper-middle-class home where Mrs. Teasdale paid hom-
age to the traditional Victorian modes of behavior with all the
strident force of her vigorous personality. Her daughter, as

---

*The lower case spelling used in this volume was the one
preferred by the poet.

a result, was to be torn for many years between a desire for the life of artistic achievement promised by her developing talent, and a fear that its pursuit would deprive her of the loving fulfillments of womanhood. Many aspects of this struggle, particularly her search for the love that would justify the giving up of the separate self, became the themes of her poetry. (Love Songs, published in 1917, is one of her best-known volumes.) Another of its emotional by-products, resentment toward the mother's imposition of her own restricted pattern, no doubt helped contribute to the habitual eruption of mild but disabling illnesses which developed as a dutiful daughter's only acceptable form of protest.

There had been much idealistic ferment over education in the city of St. Louis during the second half of the nineteenth century, and some excellent schools had been the result. Teasdale attended two of these: the Mary School, which had been founded by T. S. Eliot's father, and Hosmer Hall, where she graduated in 1903 after a solid grounding in a college preparatory curriculum administered by a largely Eastern-trained faculty. For the next ten years, the young woman traveled in this country and abroad, made contacts with other writers and editors who encouraged her, and began to publish her work. Her first pieces appeared in Reedy's Mirror (see p. 60), and in 1907 her parents underwrote the publication of her first volume of poetry: Sonnets to Duse and Other Poems. In 1910, a second volume called Helen of Troy was accepted by Putnam's, and the poet's growing reputation produced an invitation to join the Poetry Society of America.

During her twenties, Teasdale carried on correspondences with John Myers O'Hara and John Hall Wheelock, two young poets who lived in New York City. Sara's shyness made written communication appealing, but subsequent meetings with each proved her hopes for a romantic attachment ill-founded. O'Hara was unsuitable, and Wheelock did not reciprocate her strong attraction although they remained lifelong friends. Returning from Europe in the summer of 1912, a relationship was formed on shipboard with an Englishman, Stafford Hatfield, which also did not mature into the desired commitment, and sent Teasdale home to St. Louis in a temporary state of physical and emotional collapse. When the poet was almost thirty, two ardent suitors finally appeared. One was Vachel Lindsay, who had met her through Harriet Monroe, the moving spirit of the Chicago literary group (mentioned above as the editor of Poetry magazine). The other was Ernst Filsinger, a St. Louis businessman like her father, who seemed to offer the peace and security that the impoverished, labile Lindsay could not. Teasdale married Filsinger in 1914, and the marriage survived fifteen years of Sara's illnesses and Ernst's increasingly lengthy business trips. In 1929, she traveled to Reno and divorced him while he was out of the country.

Marriage, then, had proved more draining than supportive to the material and emotional life of the poet. Motherhood, too, a cherished goal of her youth, in time became threatening to Teasdale's artistic career in view of her limited strength. In 1917, after much soul-searching, she had an abortion. Not surprisingly, perhaps, the closest relationship of the last few years of her life was with a young woman named Margaret Conklin who became her literary executor, and whom Teasdale referred to as "the daughter I never had."[2] But even this tie of affection proved insufficient to maintain her in an existence increasingly beset by financial worries and the imagined threat of incapacitating illness. In 1933, just over a year after Vachel Lindsay's suicide, Sara Teasdale took an overdose of sleeping pills and ended the long struggle to create an equilibrium between the opposing tensions of her life.

Some of the contradictions of Teasdale's thinking and emotional processes emerge in the history of her relations with and comments on the other major poets of her time. Edna St. Vincent Millay was invited to tea and dinner after their meeting in 1913 (see p. 59) but a friendship failed to develop despite an exciting ride which the two women shared atop a New York City double-decker bus. Elinor Wylie's rapid rise to literary and social prominence received the following characterization: "(She) continues to climb the slopes of Parnassus before a dazzled multitude. Her work becomes more cryptic, crabbed and queer every week.... She is undoubtedly an attractive and clever person--but a great spirit? I wonder."[3] Robert Frost, too, is taken to task in another of Teasdale's letters for his "ill-temper under criticism,"[4] yet she wrote warm praise to the controversial and abrasive Amy Lowell for her Pictures of a Floating World, and went out of her way to arrange "audiences" at the two Lowell strongholds of Sevenels in Brookline (see p. 22), and New York's St. Regis hotel. Interestingly, although Amy Lowell (together with Vachel Lindsay and Edward Markham) accepted an honorary Doctor of Letters degree from Baylor University in 1920, Sara Teasdale declined, calling the process of academic investiture "flapdoodle."[5] She responded willingly, however, to another aspect of university life when she agreed to judge the Witter Bynner Undergraduate Poetry Contest of 1925. In a selection which is now part of literary history, Sara Teasdale awarded first place to a New York University student by the name of Countee Cullen.[6]

C. Day Lewis, in his Norton lectures of 1965-1966 on The Lyric Impulse has pointed out that "one effect of the liberation of poetry from music is, paradoxically, a nostalgic yearning for the partner it has lost."[7] Sara Teasdale was strongly drawn to German lieder during her days at Hosmer Hall, and, in fact, referred to her poetry as "my songs" throughout her life. In another curious correspondence to Lewis who claimed that "melody--a singing line--has always been essential to the lyrical poem,"[8] Teasdale defended traditional lyric poetry against the rising tide of Imagism and free verse by insisting that poetry traditionally needed "melody" as a means of making itself easy to remember and of communicating emotions.[9] To Louis Untermeyer's complaint that her poems did not show her intellect, she replied "my heart makes my songs, not I" and added "my mind is proud and strong enough to be silent."[10] It was a curious characterization of poetry as a catharsis of the emotions that enabled the self's higher consciousness to remain aloof and contained.

It is true that Teasdale's choice of poetic language is simple and direct and that her verses eschew the convoluted thought processes of Wylie and occasionally obscure allusions of Marianne Moore. In spite of her own beliefs, however, one senses Sara Teasdale's intellect strongly at work in the assimilation of knowledge gained through reading and experience, and its transmutation into a poetic form of considerable refinement. A case in point is her poem "There Will Be Stars," published as the title piece of the opening section in Dark of the Moon, which appeared in 1926 and contains some of her most mature work. Astronomy had been one of Teasdale's favorite academic disciplines since her girlhood, and she returned to it eagerly during a stay in Santa Barbara in 1919. It is painfully clear from her letters of this period that the stars both attracted and repelled her. "It is all ... seemingly so uselessly big" she wrote, and at the same time, "if I ever started a religion it would be star-worship."[11] As symbols of permanence in a changing universe, yet a cold mockery of human mortality, star images haunt and pervade her writing. Even her collection for children of formerly published work, the last publication during her lifetime, is

titled Stars Tonight. One of the inclusions is "There Will
Be Stars," illustrated with Dorothy P. Lathrop's delicate ink
drawing of two glowing, angelic creatures gazing toward earth
from their contiguous position in the heavens.

This poem very succinctly presents a distillate of
Teasdale's experience and conviction. In it, two stars come
together at the yearly equinox and shine on a particular earth-
ly place throughout eternity, although all trace of the lovers
who once inhabited it have long gone. It is a powerful poem,
and John Duke, who considers Sara Teasdale to be "the most
'settable' of American poets"[12] chose to make a song of it in
1951.[13] Although the entire poem is only eight lines long,
it contains three repetitions of the phrase "There will be
stars." Duke emphasizes this phrase by beginning it each
time on a weak beat and then moving, by means of a large
vocal leap, to a strong beat and lengthened note value on the
word "stars."

Example 3.1a, measures 1-3. Copyright 1953 by Boosey &
Hawkes: renewed 1981, reprinted by permission.

Example 3.1b, measures 25-27. Copyright 1953 by Boosey &
Hawkes: renewed 1981, reprinted by permission.

Example 3. 1c, measures 28-30. Copyright 1953 by Boosey & Hawkes: renewed 1981, reprinted by permission.

By choosing this metrical scheme, Duke has completely changed the original rhythmic structure of the poem, which incorporates a masterful variety of poetic feet, into a basic three stress line. But the elongated, high-pitched open vowel sound on the word "stars" with the leap that precedes it, creates a sense of distance coupled with desperate longing that is exactly analogous to the poetic thought. This is the very process of "assimilation" described by Langer (see p. 52) in which "a song conceived poetically sounds not as the poem sounds, but as the poem feels."[14]

The texture of Duke's accompaniment remains thin throughout, never expanding to more than one or two voices except for a few chordal structures to open and close the sections of the modified ABA form. The voice, thereby, retains prominence, but its occasional silences are woven through with melodic snatches from the piano's upper voice in a tight, contrapuntal framework.

Example 3. 2, measures 7-9. Copyright 1953 by Boosey & Hawkes: renewed 1981, reprinted by permission.

Use of word-painting is appropriate and skillful. The phrase "earth circles her orbit" turns in on itself in both the vocal line and accompaniment.

Example 3.3, measures 10-12. Copyright 1953 by Boosey & Hawkes: renewed 1981, reprinted by permission.

"Poised on the peak of midnight" leaps to a high G, pauses momentarily, and then descends in running stepwise motion. Throughout the song, but most insistently at the climactic moment (see Example 3.1c), Duke employs a broken arpeggio figure traveling up the keyboard which he has used elsewhere as a symbol of light but nowhere to greater effect.

Most of the writing in this setting is diatonic but there are moments of chromatic surprise. Two of these are the sidestep to an altered C sharp chord on "reach their zenith" and the raised fourth of the broken chord behind "while we sleep": a constricted harmony of Death. Duke, however,

Example 3.4, measures 31-36. Copyright 1953 by Boosey & Hawkes: renewed 1981, reprinted by permission.

does not leave it there. As the voice sustains "sleep, " the piano resolves to an E major triad which in this context is at once both peaceful and suspended, like Eternity itself (see Ex. 3. 4).

Robert Frost (1874-1963)

The life of Robert Frost is a study in paradox. Ignored for the first half of his more than four score years, he became, during the second half of his life, a world-renowned patriarch of the American literary scene. Recognized everywhere as the most characteristic of New England poets, he actually lived the first eleven years of his life in San Francisco. Even his pervading image as a blunt, plain-spoken man of the earth must be set off against the facts that he was an indifferent and not very successful farmer, who had spent three years studying the classics at Dartmouth and Harvard, and who had a long career himself as a University professor.

William Prescott Frost, Jr., the poet's father, had taken the opposite road in adopted regionalism. Born in New Hampshire, he had married Isabel Moodie, a teacher and sometime poet, and moved to San Francisco where he became editor of The Bulletin. Despite his origins, he was a strong Southern sympathizer in the Civil War, and named his son Robert Lee Frost. William Frost was a man of unstable personality, given to excessive drinking and attendant violence. Robert Frost's sister inherited his mental instability and the poet himself engaged in a lifelong struggle to control his own explosive temper.

When his father died in 1885, Robert Frost's life as a New Englander began. The Frost family moved to Lawrence, Massachusetts to make their home with Robert's paternal grandfather who tried to help the young man find himself after his graduation from high school as co-valedictorian (Elinor White, who shared the honors, later became his wife). For the next eight years, his grandfather supported him during his attendance at Dartmouth and later Harvard, helped him find jobs in between, and finally in 1900 bought him a farm in New Hampshire with the understanding that he was to live there at least ten years. By this time Robert Frost was married, and beginning to write poetry for which he could find no publisher. While struggling with this discouragement

97

and the hardships of trying to make a living from the farm, the poet also suffered the loss of a son at the age of four, and a daughter who died at birth. Indeed, of the six children born to the Frosts between 1896 and 1907, only two survived their father, as daughter Marjorie died of tuberculosis in 1934 and son Carol committed suicide in 1940.

The gloomy, difficult years came to an end when Frost sold the farm in 1912, took his family to England and at last found the recognition for his work that his own country had refused him. In London, he met all the leading poets of the times, and in 1913 was able to arrange the publication of A Boy's Will, his first volume of verse. Harriet Monroe and the rest of America now discovered him, and his poems were soon offered publication on his own side of the Atlantic. In 1915, the year of his return, Henry Holt published North of Boston and a new edition of A Boy's Will, closely followed by Mountain Interval in 1916. Now in demand as a teacher, Frost began the career which included three different periods of residence at Amherst College, and lectureships of varying lengths at Dartmouth College, the University of Michigan, Yale, Harvard, and Wesleyan universities. In 1920, he became a co-founder of the Bread Loaf School of English at Middlebury College, Vermont, and spent his summers there for many years. Among the numerous honors which came to him through the passage of time were four Pulitzer prizes, the gold medal of the Poetry Society of America, and honorary doctorates from both Oxford and Cambridge universities, which he received during a trip to England in 1957. The last years of his life introduced a final paradox when Frost, who had been a staunch conservative all his life, became the "poet laureate" of the liberal Kennedy administration and gave a moving reading of his poem, "The Gift Outright" during the inaugural ceremonies of 1961.

Like many great creative figures in the arts, Robert Frost has frustrated critics and eluded categorization. His connections to Thoreau and Emerson, he himself readily acknowledged, but the frequently mentioned kinship to E. A. Robinson is more problematic. Though the two are linked in their portrayal of New England and the peculiarities of the region, Frost strikes out on his own path to introduce new dimensions of non-literary language and, although he would certainly have protested this,[15] becomes akin to Sandburg in his attempt to capture the true sound of his own corner of America. The consummate craftsmanship with which he embedded this new language into a variety of carefully controlled poetic structures is nowhere in dispute. The "meaning" of the poetry, always of prime importance to Frost, is also now approaching consensus, as he begins to be seen as an existentialist grounded in an inscrutable God, who must summon his courage, humor, and loving ties to men and nature in order to survive the dark trials of life in this world.

John Duke recalls meeting Robert Frost in Amherst, "on which occasion a mezzo from Smith sang my settings of: 'To the Thawing Wind' and 'Acquainted with the Night.' He was very polite" said Duke, "but I could see that he had little understanding of what the art-song really is. In fact, I do not blame poets," he continued, "if they object to the composers taking their verses and using them for their own purposes, sometimes with little regard for the original form of the poem."[16] One is, in fact, reminded of Goethe, and his legendary resentment of the Schubert settings, but it is also possible that Frost may have considered the addition of music to his poetry to be superfluous rather than invasive. As early as 1915 he had expressed a conviction that the tones of actual speech are themselves musical[17] and that speech could be converted into a poetic idiom by developing "the sound of sense."[18] It is interesting that the latter concept is extremely close to ideas expressed in 1942 by T. S. Eliot,[19] for many years Frost's arch rival, as leader of the "modernist" camp, and as winner of the Nobel prize, which Frost coveted but never received.

"To the Thawing Wind" appeared in A Boy's Will, Frost's first published collection. It is written in couplets, one of the poet's favorite structures, with a rhyming line added to the last couplet, making a total of fifteen lines. There are traces of literary language, such as the contractions "o'er" and "e'er," but the blunt, compact energy of Frost is already evident in this swinging trochaic invocation to a storm. Robert Frost's concept of poetry as metaphor (to which he often referred) serves him here as the speaker is revealed to be a poet working in his "narrow stall" who should be turned "out of door": a Thoreau-esque suggestion of the need for man to become involved in nature with his senses rather than with just his intellect.

John Duke's setting of "To the Thawing Wind," written in 1951,[20] seems to bear out Philip Gerber's observation that Frost equates water with fertility and vigor in his poetry.[21] From the opening measures, the song plunges into an extremely vigorous torrent of life-giving wind and rain, embodied in an accompaniment which employs the full span of the keyboard and many of its resources of dynamics and figuration. As the storm gathers outside, the repeated broken chord structures come in rising and falling waves of sound punctuated by scale and arpeggio figures in the vocal rests.

Example 3.5, measures 5-8. Copyright © 1964, Southern Music Publishing Co., Inc.; used by permission.

With the poet's exhortation to the storm to enter his room, the pattern changes, as the words "Burst" and "Swing" are set with asymmetric accents on the weak second beat, and further dramatized by the swooping arpeggios of the accompaniment.

Example 3.6, measures 25-28. Copyright © 1964, Southern Music Publishing Co., Inc.; used by permission.

The climax of the song, "Turn the poet out of door" begins with a sustained fortissimo high G, and this exciting moment is skillfully prepared by the composer. The setting of the preceding lines ("Run the rattling pages o'er / Scatter poems on the floor") introduces a counter-melody in the piano's upper voice, which flowers during an instrumental interlude into an imitation of the opening vocal line. It is as though the storm had become the singer, and nature and poet were one.

Example 3.7, measures 35-39. Copyright © 1964, Southern Music Publishing Co., Inc.; used by permission.

101

In 1950, one year earlier, John Duke had set "Acquainted with the Night,"[22] Frost's enormously successful essay of the difficult "terza rima" form. This poem, appearing in the 1928 publication called West-Running Brook, also seems to exist on two levels of meaning. One is the common human experience of lonely, sleepless wandering through a deserted city, while the other is well described in Babette Deutsch's suggestion of a night "which is real enough but also figurative" and a city which "seems to represent some more significant, if less actual locale."[23]

Like many of the Duke songs of this period, this one also presents a characteristic accompaniment figure. In "Acquainted with the Night" it is a group of 3, 4, or 5 grace notes preceding a longer note value: a musical suggestion of walking, in which the grace notes represent the rise of the foot, and the more sustained following note, its fall to the ground.

Example 3.8, measures 25-28. Copyright © 1964, Southern Music Publishing Co., Inc.; used by permission.

The key of the song is the appropriately dark G minor, which is clear enough although not delineated by a key signature. Considerable chromaticism in the time-honored "anguish" context of the Baroque period, creates an underlying current of anxiety, which is intensified by the altered chords and suspensions of the final phrase and piano postlude (see Ex. 3.9).

In seemingly similar fashion to the song previously discussed, John Duke begins to weave a pianistic counterpoint to the vocal line near the end of the song (see Ex. 3.10). This, however, does not blossom into a transcendental moment as does its counterpart in "To the Thawing Wind." Rather, it

Example 3.9, measures 48-55. Copyright © 1964, Southern
Music Publishing Co., Inc.; used by permission.

Example 3.10, measures 39-41. Copyright © 1964, Southern
Music Publishing Co., Inc.; used by permission.

falls back to a reminiscence of the opening walking figure, as
the poet and composer quietly and wearily restate "I have been
one acquainted with the night."

"The Last Word of a Bluebird,"[24] written in 1955, is
Duke's last published Robert Frost setting. The poem comes
from Mountain Interval, which appeared shortly after the po-
et's return to America. In it, Frost demonstrates one of his
most appealing tones, falling "somewhere between the quizzical

103

and the tender,"[25] as he treats a subject which, though originally "a commonplace of the countryside now becomes illuminated by ... particularity."[26] The bluebird's last word before flying south is reported in simple, direct speech by a crow, who has been entrusted with a "goodbye" message for "Lesley": Robert Frost's daughter born in 1899, who was probably in her early teens at the time of writing. In a rare glimpse of the poet as affectionate father, the lines caution the child "to be good" and keep busy while awaiting the bird's return with the spring.

The vocal line of Duke's setting, which is dedicated to Louis Nicholas,[27] is distinguished by repetition, a mostly narrow contour, and short separated phrases in declamatory style, suggestive of crow-like squawkings.

Example 3.11, measures 4-9. Copyright © 1959, G. Schirmer, Inc.; used by permission.

Behind this, staccato chords and rapid sixteenth notes in a moving tempo create a light, teasing atmosphere (see Example 3.11).

As the song progresses, the bird's lurching, awkward

104

speech becomes more and more fixed in the triplet figures
which correspond to the poem's original anapestic feet

Example 3.12, measures 10-12. Copyright © 1959, G. Schir-
mer, Inc.; used by permission.

while the piano brings in an occasional reminiscence of the
lovely trilling of the bluebird.

Example 3.13, measures 22-24. Copyright © 1959, G. Schir-
mer, Inc.; used by permission.

Eventually, the staccato accompaniment chords give way
to more urgent figures that imitate the vocal triplets. With
rising excitement, almost like an incantation, the child's win-
ter tasks are set forth (see Ex. 3.14). And finally the composer
achieves what the poet, with only words at his disposal, is un-
able to do. He opens his melodic line to a lyrical curve and lets
the crow, for a brief, glorious moment, also become a singing
bird (see Ex. 3.15).

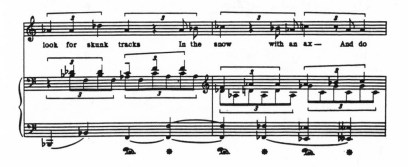

Example 3.14, measures 31-34. Copyright © 1959, G. Schirmer, Inc.; used by permission.

Example 3.15, measures 35-41. Copyright © 1959, G. Schirmer, Inc.; used by permission.

e.e. cummings (1894-1962)

It would have been surprising if e.e. cummings had not become a poet. His Cambridge childhood was spent in a big comfortable house surrounded by rose gardens and populated by loving relatives who were his playfellows and artistic companions. His father, an amateur painter, had taught sociology at Harvard before becoming a prominent Unitarian minister in Boston. (Since the elder Cummings' first name was also Edward, e.e. was known to the family by his middle name, Estlin.) His mother's love for poetry and music was absorbed by her son so quickly that at the age of three he had written his first poem, which already demonstrated in embryo cummings' new visual and aural directions.[28]

Rebecca Cummings had selected Cambridge as the place to raise Estlin and daughter Elizabeth because she felt its ambient consciousness lay between Boston's intellectual sophistication and Concord's spirituality. Nor was she mistaken, for cummings' writing career was to be equally founded in the thorough education he received at the Boston Latin School and Harvard University, and in his absorption of the Transcendental world-view. It is, of course, not unlikely that cummings' rather diffident personality was another result of his excessively protected and indulged formative years, but having raised her son to be a poet, Rebecca Cummings never withdrew her support from that enterprise. She gave him Joy Farm, the family summer retreat in New Hampshire, paid

for the printing of No Thanks (1935) when publishers refused
the collection, and sent him money every month during the
leanest times of the Depression.

It was during his Harvard years of 1911 to 1916, which
culminated in a Master of Arts degree, that e.e. cummings
turned away from the literary and artistic traditions he had
been absorbing since birth.   With growing excitement, he now
began to explore recent European movements in painting, mu-
sic, and poetry, and delivered a Commencement address on
"The New Art" which discussed the work of Cézanne, Matisse,
Stravinsky, Schoenberg, Amy Lowell, and Gertrude Stein
among others.   His mentors in this vital aspect of his edu-
cation had not been his professors.   Rather, they were class-
mates such as S. Foster Damon, editor of the Harvard Music
Review, who taught cummings to play the piano and compose
(he already played ragtime by ear); Scofield Thayer, who in-
troduced him to Joyce and Eliot; and Sibley Watson, his clos-
est lifelong friend, who brought the poetry of Verlaine and
Rimbaud to his attention.

After leaving Harvard, cummings began to consolidate
the poetic style that was to be characteristic of his future
work as he experimented with the integration of visual im-
ages and sound patterns.   He had just moved into a pleasant
Greenwich Village studio that also enabled him to develop his
talents as a painter, when he was drawn into World War I.
Waiting for assignment in Paris was the only pleasant part
of the experience.   In this city, he felt that he "participated
in an actual marriage of material and unmaterial things,"29
and he was to return there for artistic sustenance many times
during his life.

In 1919, the historic first issue of The Dial appeared
in New York with Sibley Watson as publisher, Scofield Thayer
as editor-in-chief, and Stewart Mitchell, another Harvard
classmate, as managing editor.   cummings was among the
members of the old Harvard Monthly group from whom the
editors solicited contributions, and several of his critical
pieces appeared early on as did five of his "spring" poems
in May, 1920.   He continued to write for The Dial, and other
"little magazines" through the twenties, a decade which also
saw the publication of Tulips and Chimneys (collected verse)
and a dramatic collaboration with the Provincetown Players.
cummings' personal life in these years was traumatic: his
marriage to Elaine, the divorced wife of Scofield Thayer,
ended in failure, and a daughter who never learned until

adulthood that cummings was her father. A second marriage, to Anne Barton, failed also, but by the early thirties he had come together with Marian Morehouse, an elegant fashion model and photographer, who remained a devoted wife, companion, and nurturer until his death.

In the late thirties, cummings finally gained the recognition of the literary world with the publication of Collected Poems. Awards followed, as did requests for him to read at various colleges, and in 1952-53, he held the Norton Professorship of Poetry at Harvard. cummings, who had become increasingly reactionary and reclusive after his anti-Soviet travelogue Eimi was published in 1933, consistently refused to have a radio or television set, and would have nothing to do with World War II. Despite unrelenting economic pressures and failing health, however, he continued to write poetry of remarkable vigor and freshness, even up to the last few years of his life. Having finally, in 1962, persuaded Marian to publish a volume of her photographs, he did not live to see it, but died of a cerebral hemorrhage at Joy Farm.

e.e. cummings brought a whole new battle plan to the American Revolution in poetic language which had been started by Whitman and Dickinson and carried forward in his own century by Frost and Sandburg. Now the target was no longer merely traditional literary usage, but the conventional appearance and function of words themselves. Spurred on by Dadaist scorn of pomposity and a feeling of kinship with the "little" man, [30] he adopted the lower case "i" and began to distort punctuation and syntax in an imitation of the writing style of Sam Ward, the hired man at Joy Farm. At the same time, he applied the European techniques of the Cubist painters and Webern's reductionist "Klangfarbenmelodie"[31] to a breaking apart of the formal lyric into new visual patterns. cummings' painter's eye was a vital element in the new arrangements, but his musician's ear was equally important in the free, rhythmic flow of sound sequences they embodied.

From the vantage point of the 1980's, it now begins to appear that e.e. cummings' message was slightly ahead of its historical time. His most perceptive critics have recognized the mystical implications of his poetry, and have traced the "cosmic" vocabulary with which he describes the "transcendent sphere of spiritual fulfillment central to (his) conceptual world."[32] In truth, cummings had gone beyond the twentieth century updating of Transcendentalism which is suggested by his "habit of associating love with the landscapes, the sea-

109

sons, the time of day, and with time and death. "33 With pre-Hiroshima insight, he had always distrusted the goals of science, and as time went on he became more convinced that man's intellect was the breeding ground of fear and the enemy of love. In retrospect, his cause is that of the advancing Acquarian Age whose heralds are particularly vocal in America: a rebirth into a New World which is to be reached, not in the manner of our founding fathers, but by a voyage within.

The title of Tulips and Chimneys, which in 1937 was finally issued in the entirety of its original manuscript, seems to refer to a stylistic distinction. The "tulips, " as "natural" structures, are mostly in free verse while the "chimneys" are sonnets, representing "artificial" structures. 34 "[I]n just-spring" is a "tulip"--one of five "Chansons Innocentes" which are all about children--and this is where cummings begins his experimentation with unconventional spacing and grouping of lines into stanzas. A technique that the poet would develop later--the transformation of parts of speech--is used only once here, as an adjective becomes an adverb in the sentence "the little / lame balloonman / whistles far and wee. "

The childhood that cummings celebrated in this poem was his own. On the Cambridge street where the big house stood, spring thaws always filled a low spot with a huge "mud-luscious" puddle and the "balloonman" blowing his whistle was the sure sign of the advent of the gentler season. When "eddieandbill come running from marbles and piracies" and "bettyandisbel come dancing" it is Edward Estlin himself and his sister Elizabeth who, with their companions, have been released by spring into the out-of-doors. "Just-Spring"35 was John Duke's first e. e. cummings setting (1949), and it contains musical elements which serve to capture in a remarkable fashion not only the mood of the poem but the very look and spacing of the words on the page.

The sound and "feel" of children playing in the streets is immediately established in the introduction by a "taunt" melody which runs in and out of the modulating accompaniment (see Ex. 3. 16). It frequently breaks up into smaller melodic components which skip around the keyboard in gleeful abandon (see Ex. 3. 17).

Over this background, Duke has worked out a rhythmic scheme for the vocal line which applies sustained notes to the words which are alone on their poetic lines or separated by extended spacing, and short, run-together note values for those words which are placed close to each other.

110

Example 3.16, measures 1-3.　Copyright 1954, Carl Fischer, Inc.; used by permission.

Example 3.17, measures 51-53.　Copyright 1954, Carl Fischer, Inc.; used by permission.

Thus
> "in Just-
> Spring"

becomes:

Example 3.18, measures 10-13.　Copyright 1954, Carl Fischer, Inc.; used by permission.

while

"and bettyandisbel come dancing"

takes this form:

Example 3.19, measures 54-57. Copyright 1954, Carl Fischer, Inc.; used by permission.

The setting of the

"far
and
wee"

whistling of the balloonman takes on the further aspect of musical word-painting through pitch (this is one of the "far"-thest pitches called for in a Duke song), while the dynamic indications suggest his "goat-footed" retreat down the city-street, and into the haze of his mythical origins (see Ex. 3.20).

"The Mountains are Dancing"[36] is from XAIPE, a poetry collection published in 1950 when cummings was 56. Now plagued intermittently by back pain, depressive episodes, and an increasing sense of isolation from society, he nevertheless gave the book a Greek title which translated means "rejoice." The collection is dedicated to Hildegarde Watson, who was Sibley's wife and a devoted friend to many poets.[37] It contains the full flowering of his artistry and thought, with many of the poems structured in almost conventional forms, except for the absence of capitals and some punctuation. "The

112

Mountains are Dancing" is one of these, written in three seven-line stanzas, which incorporate skillful variations of meaning and sound as well as two evolving refrains that tie the verses together.

Example 3.20, measures 68-74. Copyright 1954, Carl Fischer, Inc.; used by permission.

The Duke setting of the poem[38] (1955) is mentioned in the first volume of this series (Chapter I, p. 9) as an example of an exact rhythmic correspondence between the dactyllic poetic feet and the 3/8 musical meter which breaks the steady eighth note movement of the vocal line only at the refrains.

Example 3.21, measures 43-47. Copyright © 1956, Carl Fischer, Inc.; used by permission.

The poem is a joyous celebration of love in the human and

natural worlds, and validates "wishing, having and giving"
while it negates the "unworld" of "keeping and doubting."
Duke appropriately makes of it a rollicking dance with breath-
less, though lightly textured, accented, pianistic arpeggios
propelling the motion.

Example 3.22, measures 13-16. Copyright © 1956, Carl Fi-
scher, Inc.; used by permission.

The verbal variation is matched by musical changes in
the keys and vocal contours of each verse. The final refrain
returns to the opening key of G major with a jubilant, sustained
A on "dancing" that holds while the dance expends its final burst
of energy (see Ex. 3.23). Notice also that Duke pictorializes
the "unworld" with a descending line that derives from the word
"downward," (see Ex. 3.24) while "breathing, wishing and hav-
ing" always take on a rising sequence (see Ex. 3.22).

Eight years after XAIPE, cummings published 95 Po-
ems. Fifteen of them are love poems, and they have re-
ceived the highest critical acclaim. "The force, the depth,
and the intensity of the emotions in these poems" says Nor-

Example 3.23, measures 139-148.   Copyright © 1956, Carl
Fischer, Inc.; used by permission.

Example 3.24, measures 17-20.   Copyright © 1956, Carl Fi-
scher, Inc.; used by permission.

man Friedman, "are unmatched in all of modern poetry."[39]
Number 92 of the group is the sonnet "i carry your heart":
a full, mature expression of the poet's belief in love as a
transforming and transfiguring force in the natural world
("and it's you are whatever a moon has always meant").
"The deepest secret" and "the wonder" to which he alludes
in the third stanza refer to his further conviction that the
living world of the spirit needs the material world in order
to transcend it.[40]

For this, the last of his cummings' settings, com-
posed in 1960,[41] John Duke has restructured the sonnet's
original groupings of five-stress lines which cut across and
into verbal meanings. cummings'

> "i carry your heart with me (i carry it in
> my heart) i am never without it (anywhere"

115

becomes

Example 3.25, measures 5-11. Copyright © 1962, G. Schirmer, Inc.; used by permission.

By the third stanza, cummings' lines and meaning have grown together, but he does choose to visually separate the final line into a refrain position. This gives Duke the opportunity to compose a coda which contains reminiscences of both the principal vocal motif and recurring pianistic figurations.

Example 3.26, measures 59-66.   Copyright © 1962, G. Schirmer, Inc.; used by permission.

As can be seen from this coda, "i carry your heart" contains some of Duke's most lyrical writing for both voice

Example 3.27, measures 52-58.   Copyright © 1962, G. Schirmer, Inc.; used by permission.

117

and piano, full of melting melodic contours and warm instrumental passages of consecutive thirds. The exciting crescendo which precedes the coda is built on a series of rising chromatic sequences that culminate in the same climactic pitch (G-sharp) as in his setting of Teasdale's "There Will Be Stars. " However, cummings' affirmation of the power of love is many universes away from Teasdale's despair, and Duke's musical context makes this unerringly clear (see Ex. 3.27).

Mark Van Doren (1894-1972)

"The world, I am certain, " wrote Mark Van Doren in his autobiography, "is a terrible place, but I am just as certain that I love it.[42] ... By some odd chance, " he added, "and for no good reason, I am happy. "[43] The ability to make these statements in 1958, despite the trials and terrors of life in the twentieth century would seem in itself a remarkable accomplishment. Nor were the words those of a recluse who had retained his equilibrium through isolation and withdrawal. Rather, they came from a man who had been constantly engaged with life and people, as teacher, editor, writer, and loving member of a large family.

His earliest memories were of the Van Doren farm in Hope, Illinois, where he was "an affectionate child in an affectionate family. "[44] His father was a country doctor, and his mother an intelligent woman, devoted equally to each of her five sons, who taught Mark to read at the age of four. The house was filled with books and it was not surprising that Mark and his older brother Carl both chose to spend their lives with literature.

The family moved to Urbana when Van Doren was six, and remained there, so the choice of the University of Illinois for undergraduate studies was a natural one. By his senior year, he was editor of the Illinois Magazine, which also published his essays, one story, and a few poems. One more year of study there produced a master's degree and a thesis on Thoreau which soon found its way to publication by Houghton Mifflin, who had published the writings of Thoreau himself.

In 1915, Mark followed Carl's path to Columbia University, and began writing his doctoral dissertation on the works of Dryden--a subject also suggested by his brother. The choice was never to be regretted, for Van Doren not only came to "admire (Dryden's) music" but to believe that music to have been "the chief determining factor upon the poems I myself would write."[45] He went on to say that he would never forget the feeling for melodic structure which Dryden had given him. It is interesting to observe how often Mark Van Doren, who had studied the piano as a child and played at his brother Guy's wedding in 1910, would, along with so many other poets, describe poetry (his own and others') in terms of music.

Drafted into the infantry in World War I, he eventually received officer's training, and was so haunted by the richness of his army experiences that on his return to New York he was forced to exorcise them in a manner which became his habit: by writing an account of them. After a year of a traveling fellowship in Europe which he spent in company with his lifelong friend, Joseph Wood Krutch, he settled down in New York City and began a teaching career at Columbia which was to continue for more than thirty years.

Thomas Merton, who became a contemplative monk as well as writer, was only one of the many students whose minds flowered in the "sanity and wisdom"[46] of Mark Van Doren's classes. In his own autobiographical writing, Merton praises the simplicity and sincerity with which the professor encountered generation after generation of students, and describes the inspired questions with which he led his pupils to say "excellent things" that they did not know they knew and "had not, in fact, known before."[47] In truth, it was more than literature that was being taught, for in Van Doren's famous Shakespeare course, the discussion was really about "the deepest springs of human desire and hope and fear, ... precisely in (Shakespeare's) own terms."[48]

Teaching was not all of Van Doren's life during the Columbia years. In 1921, he married Dorothy Graffe, who was also a writer and editor. In time they had two sons, moved into a house on Bleecker Street in New York's Greenwich Village, and also bought a country place in Connecticut which was to be the setting for several fruitful sabbatical years. City and country equally enriched the spirit of this man who claimed that books and studies had never completely filled his world and that he had "loved as many things outside as in."[49] The city, to him, was "a drama, as without words

119

or music, the country is a lyric," and at the same time he perceived New York to be "a quiet place. For many," he explained, "it is not quiet, but they have not penetrated to that mysterious part of it where multiplicity, pleased with itself, lies down and dreams that it is one thing after all."[50]

Mark succeeded Carl as literary editor of the Nation (1924-1928) and served the publication for three years in the middle thirties as film critic. His editing talents were also put to use in a number of anthologies, notably the Oxford Book of American Prose and the Anthology of World Poetry. The latter is an impressive collection of fine translations chosen by a discerning ear which had been honed not only by long devotion to reading and teaching poetry, but by writing vast amounts of his own. In a letter to John Duke, written in 1971, one year before his death, Van Doren describes himself as still pursuing his favorite occupation of "reading several anthologies of English poems.... When I do that," he tells the composer, "certain lyrics sing out. They are more than words; they are music. Not music with notes-- or yes, with notes, and the notes are the words."[51]

There are many parallels between the lives of John Duke and Mark Van Doren. Both had long rewarding teaching careers at major Eastern centers of higher education; both had stable marriages to women named Dorothy who were writers; and both used the relative protection of the academic environment to permit an enormous flowering of lifelong creativity. It was predictable that a warm friendship would result when the Van Dorens called on the Dukes, the morning after Mark Van Doren had given a lecture on Shakespeare at Smith College. "It was a most memorable visit," writes Duke. "He was most enthusiastic about my settings of his poetry and from then on we kept up quite a frequent correspondence.... I have always regretted that I never got around to accepting his urgent invitation to visit him at his home in Falls Village, Connecticut. For he was one of the most charming personalities I have ever encountered."[52]

The first collection of the hundreds of poems Mark Van Doren was to write, appeared in 1924 under the title of its opening lyric: Spring Thunder. Critics called them "country poems" and aligned him with Robert Frost.[53] As Van Doren pointed out in his autobiography, "country poems" were certainly a category that he had never ceased to write, but that it had been only one among many. "Spring Thunder" is a powerful treatment, in three, short four-line stanzas, of the moment just before a thunderstorm breaks on a warm night in the awakening season. John Duke's song by the same name, [54] written in 1960, is an equally terse two-page setting which allows very little in the way of sustained notes or piano interludes to interrupt the headlong moment of the storm's approach.

Written in the midst of a period of songs with relatively quiet, chordal accompaniments, this song brings back more elaborate pianistic figures: rising arpeggios which suggest the sky's eerie, ascending glow of warmth and light, and the pounding broken octaves of nature's menace.

Example 3.28a, measures 9-12. Copyright © 1968, Carl Fischer, Inc.; used by permission.

Example 3.28b, measures 16-18. Copyright © 1968, Carl Fischer, Inc.; used by permission.

Diminished chords predominate in the accompaniment harmonies and are outlined in the vocal line, creating a sense of unease throughout. By contrast, the major triads which do occur have a comforting aural effect appropriate to the setting of such phrases as "it is warm,"--the verbal acknowledgement of fierce winter's slackening (see Example 3.28a). The final line of the song is a masterful instrumental representation of the barely audible moment in which the "edge of winter" begins to "crumble." This is followed by a whispered vocal speculation on the event, whose echo of the foregoing diminished chord carries a suggestion of doubtful hope.

Example 3.29, measures 23-28. Copyright © 1968, Carl Fischer, Inc.; used by permission.

Through the years when Mark Van Doren was in demand on the lecture circuit, he managed to schedule many side trips back to Urbana, usually by train. The poems he wrote while riding these trains became the group called "In that Far Land," which were published in the collection Spring Birth (1953). The distance separating him from that land was not geographical. Rather, it was far off in time: the world of the poet's childhood, and the poem "Only for Me" recreated one of its most poignant memories. Beth Knowlton, a girl who had captured Mark's twelve-year old heart, had been reported by brother Frank to have been seen with another boy. Van Doren crystallized the unforgettably painful jealousy he experienced in a poem called "Only for Me," which changed the sufferer into a girl named Linda Jane who wept and died for him in a youthful dream.

The song, "Only for Me,"[55] written in 1954, was actually John Duke's first Van Doren setting. In it, the composer's fluidity of harmonic rhythm suggests the emotional lability of the adolescent protagonist, while the high tessitura and leaping contour of the vocal line adds the breathless awkwardness of the age.

Example 3.30, measures 11-16. Copyright 1955, Boosey &
Hawkes, Inc.; used by permission.

The truly magical moment of this setting derives from the last
line of verse two: "Weeping everywhere like rain." The voice
having made a stifled, wondering leap of an octave, the piano
then takes over in a spilling torrent of tears (see Ex. 3.31).
The memory of this emotion, symbolized by the piano figures
of broken sixteenth notes, continues behind the "sunrise," and
the "growing up" as a dream lingers into waking. It stops,
musically as well, only with "the forgetting" (see Ex. 3.32).

In New Poems (1948), there is a group which Van
Doren called "Words for Music, More or Less." Of these,
the poet wrote "a number of poems in the section were sub-
sequently set to music as I had hoped they would be....
Nothing pleases me more than that."[56] Among this group
is "One Red Rose," a celebration of a long lasting love "that
lives / When nothing else does any longer." The poet's trib-
ute to his life's companion became the composer's as well
with John Duke's setting written in 1964,[57] the forty-second
anniversary year of a marriage which was to end only with
Mrs. Duke's death in 1977. Again, as in the cummings love
song, "i carry your heart," a sweepingly lyrical vocal line
is emphasized. Surrounding, supporting and entwining with this
line is a lush, melodic counterpoint in the piano (see Ex. 3.33).

123

Example 3.31, measures 35-41. Copyright 1955, Boosey & Hawkes, Inc.; used by permission.

Example 3.32, measures 48-50. Copyright 1955, Boosey & Hawkes, Inc.; used by permission.

For the final phrases of the song, the counter-melody ceases, so as to concentrate attention on the vocal suspensions which highlight the words "loving" and "true" (see Ex. 3.34).

Joseph Wood Krutch was of the opinion that all Van Doren's poems are love poems. This writer agrees, and

Example 3.33, measures 34-39.   Copyright © 1970, Carl Fischer, Inc.; used by permission.

Example 3.34, measures 61-68.   Copyright © 1970, Carl Fischer, Inc.; used by permission.

finds, furthermore, that the passion of the poet increases and the expression of it gains compression and force in the late poetry as mortality threatens an end to feeling and perception. "O, World," the first of the Late Poems published in 1963 contains two verses whose lines lack Van Doren's usual regularity of length and meter, as though emotion had shattered form. John Duke, in his 1965 setting of "O, World,"[58] translated this loosening of constraint into great keyboard-spanning instrumental figurations.

Example 3.35, measures 3-6. Copyright © 1970, Carl Fischer, Inc.; used by permission.

The passion ebbs and flows at rising and falling pitch levels with varied rhythmic groupings of notes per beat. "O Stillness" takes on an element of mystery by virtue of its enharmonic vocal derivation, while the contrasting, and final, "O great sky," has dramatically expansive cluster chords, and a sustained fortissimo vocal tone that suggests the reaches of the universe and the human heart.

Example 3.36, measures 47-56. Copyright © 1970, Carl Fischer, Inc.; used by permission.

Emily Dickinson (1830-1886)

The reader is referred to Volume I, chapter four, of this series, for material on Emily Dickinson in connection with settings of her poetry by Ernst Bacon and Aaron Copland. Curiously enough, it was not until 1968, that John Duke chose to deal with her work in the Six Poems by Emily Dickinson, [59] by which time one hundred and forty-three of his songs had preceded them. This fact is surprising, at least partly be-

127

cause of Northampton's close proximity to Amherst, which contains the Dickinson family home and Amherst College, the latter founded largely through the efforts of Emily's grandfather at a ruinous cost to his own fortunes. Eventually, however, Duke did become involved with this nerve-center of the Dickinson legend, and he describes a meeting with Martha Dickinson Bianchi, the poet's niece, that occurred when he played the organ for a service in the Congregational Church just down the street from Emily's house. It might also be noted that the cover of John Duke's recording with Carole Bogard, soprano (which contains a sensitive performance of the Six Poems) displays a photograph of the singer and composer with the imposing Dickinson Homestead (as it was called) in the background.

Having come to this poetry late in his composing career, Duke had the advantage of the complete Thomas H. Johnson edition, which had been unavailable to Bacon and Copland and other composers setting her work before the edition's appearance in 1955. Duke has studied these volumes as well as a whole shelf of critical and biographical works on Emily Dickinson which he keeps in his upstairs study. He speaks of "the controversy over her poetry" and the fact that "some of it is hard to decipher (since) parts of the Johnson collection are only scraps,"[60] but professes great admiration for many of the verses, particularly the ones he has set.

Recent scholarship, notably that of Richard B. Sewall,[61] has drawn together the extensive Dickinson research of the past several decades into a newly comprehensive synthesis. The picture that now emerges is no longer that of a reclusive martyr to an early episode of unrequited love. Indeed there is considerable evidence pointing to the poet's deep emotional involvement with both Samuel Bowles, editor of the Springfield Republican, and Judge Otis Lord of Salem, in the years following her conjectural attachment to the Rev. Charles Wadsworth which has never received documentary support. Many other devotions of the heart, to friends and family members, to Amherst and her family home, are also now clearly seen to have loomed large in her existence, but the principal counter-subject to love in Dickinson's life seems, constantly and tragically, to have been loss. With many girlhood friends and with Susan Gilbert, her brother's wife, the loss appears in the form of rejection by those whose spirits were not equal to the floodtides of the poet's affections. With the men to whom she gave her passion, all married and therefore unattainable, the loss was implicit at the outset. But the supreme agent of loss, and the enemy who most engaged her, was Death, whose strokes separated her throughout her life from many she held dear including her beloved nephew, Gilbert, who died at the tender age of nine.

Gradually, as the losses accumulated, and as Dickinson began to realize how removed she was, intellectually and spiritually, from the simplistic pietism and the literary traditions of her environment, it became easier to live in her own world, inside the home that she always perceived as a haven of peace and beauty. The Six Poems that John Duke set have been given dates by Johnson which place them between 1858 and 1865: years of great upheaval in Emily's life, during which these patterns of withdrawal were being set in motion. This was the period of Samuel Bowles' visits to the Dickinson home, and of his departure for Europe. It was also a time of anxiety over her mother's health, her brother's marriage, her sister's ill-fated love affair and her own threatened loss of sight; all of which were compounded by the failure to evoke understanding of her work from Higginson, the short-sighted editor of the Atlantic Monthly, whose advice she had sought. Of the six poems, three clearly stem from the sorrows of her life and her ambivalent feelings about Death, while the other three arise out of her strong ties to Nature, always one of her greatest comforters.

The contrast in the poetry occasions equal contrast in the settings, which are, in general, quite different in style from the musical expansiveness of the Duke songs that immediately preceded them.[62] Most of the writing is fairly thin in texture and mirrors the qualities of intimacy and simplicity with which Emily cut through the lush posturing of the Romantic age. The first poem, "Good morning, Midnight" (1862) is a delicately restrained lament by the writer over her need to remain in the figurative darkness of midnight, since she has been rejected by "day" and "sunshine" and all the brightness of life. The setting is quite transparent, with an uncluttered piano part that affords prominence to the vocal line. The latter is divided into short, broken-up phrases which seem to derive from the last couplet

> "But-please take a little Girl--
> He turned away!"

and lend a child-like atmosphere to the song (see Ex. 3.37).

Number two, "Heart! We will forget him!" (written

Example 3.37, measures 24-27. Copyright © 1978, Southern
Music Publishing Co.; used by permission.

in 1858) presents a very different concept of this poem from the
familiar Copland setting, and also employs the more authentic
Johnson version of the poetry, which changes the sixth line from

<blockquote>"That I my thoughts may dim"</blockquote>

to

<blockquote>"That I may straight begin."</blockquote>

Unlike the nostalgic reminiscence of the earlier setting, John
Duke's is rooted in agitation and anguish. The rushing pianistic
triplets and an opening vocal leap of an octave clearly portray the
active pain which belies the poet's exhortation to forget.

Example 3.38, measures 1-2. Copyright © 1978, Southern
Music Publishing Co.; used by permission.

The third song, "Let down the bars, Oh Death," is a
quiet pause between the storms of two and four. The 1865
poem portrays Death as a haven of release for "the tired
flocks ... whose wandering is done"--an idea which Emily
Dickinson struggled all her life to accept with varying suc-
cess. Duke suggests this procession of weary souls with a
tranquillo tempo, ceremonial 5/4 meter, and a succession of
widely spaced piano chords in C sharp minor.

Example 3.39, measures 1-3. Copyright © 1978, Southern
Music Publishing Co.; used by permission.

This is followed by a keyboard interlude whose pianissimo
dynamic level and turn to the major mode establish the sec-
ond verse's view of Death as a quiet, welcome comforter.

Example 3.40, measures 10-15. Copyright © 1978, Southern
Music Publishing Co.; used by permission.

The vocal leap to a soft, high, sustained tone on "tender,"
is the emotional climax of the song, and a perfect musical
counterpart of the poet's notion of something that (if true) is
too precious "to be told."

Example 3.41, measures 20-22. Copyright © 1978, Southern
Music Publishing Co.; used by permission.

"An awful Tempest mashed the air" is from 1860, and
in this poem, Dickinson sees her beloved Nature briefly in-
habited by demonic "creatures" who "chuckled on the Roofs
... and swung their frenzied hair." The tempest, one feels,
may well be symbolic of an inner storm, but by the end of
verse three, "peace" like "Paradise" has returned to the in-
ner and outer atmosphere. This is the most dynamic setting
of the six, with its agitato piano prelude and interludes, and

the unusual 5/8 4/8 meter creating a sense of the storm's uneven gusting.

Example 3.42, measures 1-6. Copyright © 1978, Southern Music Publishing Co.; used by permission.

The final verse, when calm returns with morning, receives a lento setting, and bears some similarity to the tolling of the morning bells in the final section of Hugo Wolf's "In der Fruehe."

The fifth poem, "Nobody knows this little Rose," carries the date of 1858 (actually the earliest year assigned by Johnson to any in the collection) and shows Dickinson, from the outset, giving literary form to her obsession with the impermanence of life and beauty. Here the subject is a flower, observed no doubt in her garden, which was one of Dickinson's chief sources of pleasure throughout her life. "Only a breeze" she says "will sigh" at the death of this little rose, and the reader assumes an intimated analogy to the scarcely marked passing from the physical world of all individual forms of life. John Duke's setting of the poem is the most lyrical of the six, and shows the heavy employment of consecutive

133

thirds in the piano writing that the composer usually reserves for love songs in the conventional sense.

No - bo - dy knows   this   lit - tle rose

Example 3.43, measures 1-6. Copyright © 1978, Southern Music Publishing Co.; used by permission.

The flexible harmonic movement with which Duke typically alights in a rapid succession of tonal areas is especially appropriate here in its suggestion of the busy movements of "bee," "bird," and "butterfly." The poignancy of the final couplet

> "Ah, Little Rose--how easy
> For such as thee to die!"

derives, in the setting, largely from the pianistic melody, with its grieving chordal appogiaturas, that fills in the vocal hold on "thee," and then repeats softly in augmentation in the brief postlude (see Ex. 3.44).

The final song sets "Bee! I'm expecting you!," a three verse poem of great charm from 1865, written in the form of a letter signed "Yours, Fly," which describes the

Example 3.44, measures 27-34. Copyright © 1978, Southern Music Publishing Co.; used by permission.

busy springtime activities of all natural creation. Duke's setting is a masterpiece of musical word-painting in which small darting and buzzing creatures of the insect world are suggested in the piano by staccato tones and rapid, chromatic scale figures blurred by the pedal:

135

Example 3.45, measures 1-6. Copyright © 1978, Southern Music Publishing Co.; used by permission.

Between these figures lie short, disconnected vocal phrases-- the excited gasps of the fly as he alights for brief, breathless moments.

136

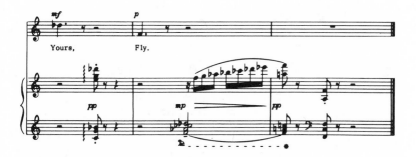

Example 3.46, measures 31-36. Copyright © 1978, Southern Music Publishing Co.; used by permission.

NOTES

1. The source of the following biographical material is Williams Drake, Sara Teasdale, Woman and Poet (San Francisco: Harper and Row, 1979). This is the first work on Teasdale to make use of hitherto unavailable materials which have now been released by Margaret Conklin, her literary executor.

2. Marya Zaturenska, "Foreword--The Strange Victory of Sara Teasdale," Collected Poems of Sara Teasdale (New York: MacMillan, 1971), p. xxxi).

3. Letter to Jessie Rittenhouse, Teasdale's friend (see p. 59). Quoted in Drake, p. 214.

4. Ibid., p. 201.

5. Ibid., p. 194.

6. See American Art Song and American Poetry, vol. I, p. 107, for material on Countee Cullen.

7. C. Day Lewis, The Lyric Impulse (Cambridge: Harvard University Press, 1965), p. 18.

8. Ibid., p. 19.

9. Drake, p. 158.

10. Ibid., p. 185.

11. Ibid., p. 222.

12. Letter to the author, dated June 25, 1982.

13. John Duke, "There Will Be Stars" (New York: Boosey & Hawkes, 1953). Medium high voice. Range: b to G sharp^2. Out of print. Held by University of North Carolina music library.

14. Langer, Feeling and Form, p. 159.

15. As clearly revealed by his disparaging comments in the published letters, Frost was jealous of Carl Sandburg and looked upon him as a rival.

16. Letter to the author, dated October 22, 1981.

17. See American Art Song and American Poetry, vol. I, p. 12, for a discussion of Sidney Lanier's quite similar theories.

18. Lawrence B. Holland, "Robert Frost," The Norton Anthology of American Literature, Vol. 2 (New York: W. W. Norton, 1979), p. 1101.

19. See American Art Song and American Poetry, vol. I, p. 15, for a discussion of T. S. Eliot's, The Music of Poetry.

20. John Duke, "To the Thawing Wind" (New York: Southern Music Publishing, 1964). Medium voice. Range: c^1 to g^2.

21. Philip L. Gerber, Robert Frost (Boston: Twayne, 1966), p. 160.

22. John Duke, "Acquainted with the Night" (New York: Southern Music Publishing, 1964). Medium voice. Range: b to f^2.

23. Deutsch, p. 80.

24. John Duke, "The Last Word of a Bluebird" (New York: G. Schirmer, 1949). Medium voice. Range: a to f^2. Out of print. Held by the University of North Carolina music library.

25. Deutsch, p. 83.

26. Ibid., p. 67.

27. Louis Nicholas has had a long career as professor of voice at George Peabody College for Teachers in Nashville, Tennessee (recently merged with Vanderbilt University). He has also held prominent positions with the National Association of Teachers of Singing, including his current chairmanship of the editorial board of the NATS Bulletin.

28. The poem was as follows:

"O, the pretty birdie, O
With his little toe, toe, toe!"

29. Charles Norman, e.e. cummings, The Magic-Maker (New York: Duell, Sloan and Pearce, 1964), p. 63.

30. Richard S. Kennedy, Dreams in the Mirror (New York: Liveright, 1980), p. 110. Kennedy points out that e.e. cummings, being small compared to his father, probably identified with the less powerful of the world.

31. "Klangfarbenmelodie" is literally tone-color melody. It refers to Webern's technique of distributing small sections of a melodic line to a number of different orchestral instruments.

32. Norman Friedman, e.e. cummings, The Art of His Poetry (Baltimore: The Johns Hopkins Press, 1960), p. 67.

33. Ibid., p. 28.

34. Norman Friedman, e.e. cummings, The Growth of a Writer (Carbondale, Ill.: Southern Illinois University Press, 1964), p. 38.

35. John Duke, "Just-Spring" (New York: Carl Fischer, 1954). High voice. Range: d^1 to b flat^2.

36. The poem itself is untitled, marked only by the number 67--a frequent practice of cummings. "The Mountains Are Dancing" is actually John Duke's title.

37. See Chapter I, p. 31.

38. John Duke, "The Mountains Are Dancing" (New York: Carl Fischer, 1956). High voice. Range: d^1 to a^2.

39. Friedman, The Growth of a Writer, p. 170.

40. Ibid., p. 7.

41. John Duke, "i carry your heart" (New York: G. Schirmer, 1962). Medium high voice. Range: c^1 to g sharp^2.

42. Mark Van Doren, The Autobiography of Mark Van Doren (New York: Harcourt, Brace, 1958), p. 348.

43. Ibid., p. 351.

44. Ibid., p. 3.

45. Ibid., p. 99.

46. Thomas Merton, The Seven Storey Mountain (New York: Harcourt, Brace, 1948), p. 179.

47. Ibid., p. 139.

48. Ibid., p. 180.

49. Van Doren, Autobiography, p. 61.

50. Ibid., p. 174.

51. Letter to John Duke from Mark Van Doren, dated February 11, 1971.

52. Letter to the author, dated October 22, 1981.

53. This comparison was probably unwelcome to Van Doren who on page 170 of his autobiography describes Frost's cynical and "devastating sentiments about the profession we shared" (i.e., teaching).

54. John Duke, "Spring Thunder" (New York: Carl Fischer, 1968). High voice. Range: e flat^1 to g^2.

55. John Duke, "Only for Me" (New York: Boosey & Hawkes, 1955). Medium voice. Range: c^1 to g^2. Out of print. Held by the Duke University music library.

56. Van Doren, Autobiography, p. 290.

57. John Duke, "One Red Rose" (New York: Carl Fischer, 1970). Medium voice. Range: b flat to f^2.

58. John Duke "O World" (New York: Carl Fischer, 1970). Medium voice. Range: d¹ to f².

59. John Duke, Six Poems by Emily Dickinson (New York: Southern Music Publishing, 1978). Soprano. Range: c¹ to a².

60. Conversation with John Duke, July 30, 1982.

61. Richard B. Sewall, ed., Emily Dickinson, A Collection of Critical Essays (Englewood Cliffs, N.J.: Prentice-Hall, 1963).

_____, The Lyman Letters--New Light on Emily Dickinson and Her Family (Amherst: The University of Massachusetts Press, 1965).

_____, The Life of Emily Dickinson (New York: Farrar, Straus and Giroux, 1974).

62. Parts of the following discussion are taken from the author's review of the Six Poems which appeared in the NATS Bulletin, vol. XXXV: 3, pp. 38-39.

IV. INTO THE NEW CENTURY

The four composers whose works will be discussed in this chapter were all born during the first decade of the twentieth century. Not surprisingly, their paths on occasion crossed or formed parallels during their musical training and careers; three of them, in fact, were students together at Juilliard in the early thirties. Further, the names of Rubin Goldmark, Nadia Boulanger, and Roger Sessions will be seen to recur in their various biographies as favored teachers of composition, and most of the four became, in time, themselves teachers to the next generation.

There are, however, marked differences among them in regard to the position of songs in their body of composition, ranging from Ross Lee Finney whose solo songs represent relatively few opus numbers in a catalog heavy with instrumental and choral works, to Sergius Kagen who wrote nothing but songs and operas. The origins of these men also demonstrate a variety befitting the American melting pot. Two are native born, but separated by the geography and traditions that lie between the northeast and midwest. Two are European-born yet adapt so quickly to the new culture that there remains no question of their status as American composers.

Finally, one might observe the uneven workings of destiny in the varying lengths of their careers. Ross Lee Finney, the oldest, is alive and active at this writing, Sergius Kagen and Paul Nordoff died of natural causes at the ages of 55 and 67 respectively, while Charles Naginski was killed in a tragic accident at 31, in the early flowering of his impressive talent. Since three out of the four composers were born in 1909, those will be discussed (after Ross Lee Finney) according to the chronological order of their dates of death, beginning with the ill-fated Naginski.

Ross Lee Finney (1906-   )
Benjamin Franklin (1706-1790)[1]

Ross Lee Finney was born in Wells, Minnesota and as a boy studied both the cello and the piano. By the age of twelve he was proficient enough to perform as cellist with a piano trio in various small Midwestern communities. Entering the University of Minnesota in 1924, he continued to study the cello, and began composition lessons as well, with Donald Ferguson as his first instructor. Finney completed his Bachelor of Arts degree at Carleton College between 1925 and 1927, and remained there for a short time teaching cello and music history. Then a Johanson Fellowship made possible a year of study in Paris with Nadia Boulanger, after which he spent 1928 and 1929 at Harvard University taking the classes of Edward Burlingame Hill.

In the fall of 1929, Finney began his long, illustrious career of teaching in the colleges and universities of the United States. He taught at Smith College from 1929 to 1947 and during his tenure founded the Smith College Music Archives and the Valley Music Press. Remarkably, he also found the time to serve concurrently on the faculties of nearby Mt. Holyoke College (1938-40), Hartt School of Music (1941-42) and Amherst College (1946-47). World War II took him away from the campus from 1943 to 1945 for service with the Office of Strategic Services in Paris, during which time he was injured near the front and received the Purple Heart and Certificate of Merit. Thereafter reestablished at Smith College, he was, in 1948, appointed composer-in-residence and subsequently chairman of the Department of Composition at the University of Michigan in Ann Arbor, where he in time created an electronic music laboratory. His teaching career, which touched the lives of many younger composers, performers, and professors all over the country, had been interrupted by his own studies with Alban Berg[2] in Vienna (1931) and Francesco Malipiero in Venice (1937). During the thirties and forties, he had also worked with Roger Sessions on contemporary techniques which assumed increasing importance in his composition.

143

Another important association begun in the thirties was Finney's relationship with the American poet Archibald MacLeish. The composer's interest in English language text setting is traceable to this point in his career, and by 1960 he had set the poetry of MacLeish in five works: Poems by Archibald MacLeish (1935) for solo voice, Bleheris (1937) for tenor and orchestra, and the choral pieces Pole Star for This Year (1939), Words to be Spoken (1946), and Edge of Shadow (1959).

Finney's Venetian studies in 1937 had been facilitated by a Guggenheim fellowship, and a Pulitzer traveling fellowship. In 1947, he spent another year as a Guggenheim fellow composing in Claremont, California, so that Mrs. Finney, who was an authority in certain aspects of seventeenth-century literature and musicology, could use the Huntington library. During that year, Ross Lee Finney endeared himself to the Scripps College community by playing in amateur chamber music sessions, singing his folk-ballad repertoire to his own guitar accompaniment, and addressing a Scripps Convocation on "Music and the Human Need." Claremont, then, was a natural choice for Finney's return in the late fifties, on leave from the University of Michigan, to compose a symphony commissioned by the Koussevitzky foundation. Once again he delivered an address at Scripps College, this time on "Analysis and the Creative Process," an illuminating explication of the composer's working methods which was thereafter published in the College Bulletin. Said Finney on this occasion,

> My own music seems to start with a sense of gesture which must be translated at some moment into musical notes before the creative process begins. . . . I would have to define a gesture as being movement, up or down, within time and conveying some expressive idea. . . . While I must agree that leaving my desk is usually an escape from work, sometimes in the course of the excitement that forces me to move around in my studio, a sense of gesture is born. [3]

Ross Lee Finney, as just demonstrated, is a gifted writer like his erstwhile Smith College colleague, John Duke (see p. 49). In numerous journal articles such as "Composer in Residence"[4] and "The Composer in Academia,"[5] he has appeared as spokesman for those musicians who are pursuing combined careers as creators and instructors. In another, titled "Employ the Composer," he argues for the uniqueness of the composer's contribution to the college musical curriculum since "the composer does more than clarify musical practice; he evolves it."[6] He states his further belief "that the function of the composer in education (is) to upset the apple cart ... (a function) that should be valued and not feared, for the natural direction of the status quo ... is down."[7] "Theory in a Period of Change" finds him encouraging teachers of this discipline not to "accept the negative position of the reactionary or the advance guard" which would have the effect of turning the student "back into the museum or ... loose without understanding in a chaotic world. He (the student) deserves," says Finney, "a positive pedagogy, one that will establish his position in the chain of history and at the same time develop his creative imagination for the possibilities of the future."[8]

In Finney's own composition, the "possibilities of the future" came to mean a turn toward serial techniques. No doubt as a partial result of his studies with Boulanger, Berg, and Sessions and coinciding with his appointment at the University of Michigan, he began to explore the idea of reconciling tone-rows with larger designs of organization, while maintaining an "essential lyricism that is a constant (even) in the 12-tone compositions."[9] Paradoxically, his path toward dodecaphony had begun with links to the "chain of history" that extended well back into the past of Western music in general, and American music in particular. A strong interest in seventeenth-century music during the 1930's had produced Three Seventeenth Century Lyrics[10] for voice and piano, and the Finney family's custom of singing folk songs not only gave the composer his life-long avocation, but had direct influence on a number of works in his catalog.[11] His creative curiosity also excited by the musical heritage of the New England colonies, Finney composed an orchestral piece in 1943 called Hymn, Fuging and Holiday based on a hymn tune by William Billings,[12] and a choral work in 1945, Pilgrim's Psalms, which drew on melodies from the Ainsworth psalter of the Puritans.[13]

The stage, then, had been appropriately set for the appearance in 1946 of Poor Richard,[14] Ross Lee Finney's masterful cycle based on texts by Benjamin Franklin. Immersed as he was at that time in colonial life of the eighteenth century, it is not surprising that the composer was captivated by the mind and writings of one of America's greatest geniuses, whose birth coincidentally preceded Finney's by exactly two hundred years. Born in Boston and destined to staggering achievements in the arts, sciences, and world of diplomacy, the young Franklin had begun his writing career at the age of seven, with ballads which were ridiculed by his father. Josiah Franklin, a candlemaker by trade, wanted his sons to prosper in the world, and marking the impoverished condition of many educated men, set about discouraging Ben's intellectual proclivities, decided against sending him to college, and apprenticed him to his brother as a printer when he was twelve years old.

During the next five years, Franklin not only learned the printer's trade well enough to retire on its profits in 1748, but also occupied every leisure moment in a remarkably effective self-education. By the age of sixteen, he had polished his manners and his writing style and began to have accepted for publication letters which he had submitted to the New England Courant (his brother's periodical) under the pen name of Silence Dogood. The hoax eventually revealed, it became apparent that Ben's abilities needed more space in which to develop. He left Boston and his indentureship to settle, after arduous travels, into a printing job in Philadelphia, a city that reflects his influence in its intellectual life and political institutions to this day.

Franklin's next appearance as a writer occurred in London, where he had arrived in 1724 only to find himself stranded by unfulfilled promises of support from the governor of Pennsylvania. Once again he found work as a printer, and began to attract some notice in that sophisticated city with the Dissertation on Liberty and Necessity which he wrote, printed, and published. Back in Philadelphia in 1726, he was soon in business for himself, and the next year organized a group of young, poor, and enterprising Philadelphians in a society known as the Junto. This group's aims included both conviviality and philosophy, required the members to produce essays four times a year, and occasioned the writing of some of Franklin's liveliest drinking songs during its thirty year existence.

The next few years were ones of remarkable achievement for a young man in his mid-twenties. In 1729, Franklin founded the Pennsylvania Gazette, which he served in the capacities of both writer and printer. In 1730, he became the official printer for the state of Pennsylvania, and in the same year began his long, rewarding marriage to Deborah Read, a stabilizing force in the life of this man whose only passion not entirely under rationalistic control was his strong attraction to women. The year 1733 was one of the most meaningful in Franklin's career, for it saw the first publication in the Poor Richard's almanac series--a venture which was to bring him fame and fortune (by 1748 it was selling 10,000 copies annually) and provide the perfect medium for his simultaneous functions as philosopher, journalist, and (particularly germane to our purposes) balladeer and poet.

Although there had been several models for the name and format of his almanac, the humorous, homely essence of Poor Richard was Franklin's invention. In his early, livelier years, Poor Richard was by no means always on the side of prudence and calculation and spoke often of women with alternating cynicism and tenderness. The sources of his wit and wisdom were lodged in many literary masters and popular adages, and in numerous languages as well, for Franklin had, beginning in 1732, acquired a reading knowledge of French, Italian, Spanish, and German as well as his Latin of earlier acquisition. All the rich store of the author's literary acquaintance and incisive thinking was combed and adapted to suit his purpose and audience which in eighteenth century Philadelphia consisted mostly of immigrants looking for miracles and sudden riches. Poor Richard with "much wit and charm" educated them to the realization that "they must work to be happy, and save to be secure" and that "industry and frugality were the simple, natural roads to freedom."[15]

Says Ross Lee Finney of his Franklin settings, "Poor Richard reflects my love of early Americana. They were influenced by Francis Hopkinson[16] (especially the drinking song) and by the ballad songs of the 18th century."[17] In truth, it seems highly appropriate to set these texts in a style reminiscent of the period in which they were written since Franklin himself was a man strongly connected to the music of his time having learned to play the harp, guitar, and violin, as well as the glass harmonica (an instrument which he substantially improved in 1762). At meetings of the Junto, he had often taken his turn in singing, on some of these occasions writing words for already familiar airs. It is also more than likely that he composed a number of his own tunes, quite possibly for some of the texts which appear in this cycle.

Of the seven songs in Finney's Poor Richard, only three (numbers 3, 5, and 6) actually employ texts drawn from the almanac. Number one, called "Epitaph," establishes the tone of the cycle both philosophically and musically as it sets

the most famous of American epitaphs which Ben Franklin
composed for himself in 1728. Humorously employing the
language of his trade, the author states his belief that "the
body of B. Franklin, printer," though presently "Food for
Worms," will eventually appear "In a new and more elegant
Edition / Revised and corrected, / By the Author." The
vigorous, optimistic Deism of the writer is well matched by
a musical style that has been aptly characterized as "force-
ful (and) masculine ... in a music distinctly tonal, rhyth-
mically energetic, and neo-classic in formal principle."[18]
This style pervades the cycle, and the "Epitaph" performs
a unifying function by stating the rising and falling groups of
scale tones that will recur as a motto throughout the work.

Example 4.1, measures 1-4. Copyright 1950, G. Schirmer,
Inc.; used by permission.

        The key of this opening song is E minor, which Finney
first employs in its natural form, giving the beginning phrases
an ambiguous modal atmosphere (see Example 4.1). Soon, he
moves through the melodic minor and further tonal alterations
to a cadence on D major, in an expanded pandiatonicism (see
Chapter I, note 28). This procedure, together with the many
dissonant non-chord tones (found throughout the cycle) are
strongly reminiscent of Stravinsky in his neo-classic period.

Example 4.2, measures 15-25. Copyright 1950, G. Schirmer, Inc.; used by permission.

A fanciful interlude in the primarily syllabic vocal setting is the "elegant" melisma which Finney assigns to that word in the text. A recognizable link in the musical "chain of history" (see p. 145), it seems to look both in a backward direction toward the virtuosic embellishments of Baroque opera, as well as forward (from the eighteenth century) to Bellini's fioratura.

Example 4.3, measures 41-45. Copyright 1950, G. Schirmer, Inc.; used by permission.

The second setting, "Here Skugg Lies," is of another epitaph. This one was written forty-four years later during the period when Franklin, now wealthy and retired from business, served the colonies as diplomatic representative to England, the mother country whose apron strings he would soon help to untie. In 1772, the date of this writing, Franklin was a frequent visitor at Twyford, the home of Jonathan Shipley, the Bishop of Asaph. The Bishop had a son and five daugh-

149

ters and Franklin, a favorite with them all, had imported a grey squirrel from Philadelphia as a present for the girls. Skugg (which was a common English pet name for squirrels) had gotten out of his cage and been killed by dogs. The grieving children asked their benefactor to write an epitaph for Skugg's grave in the garden, and Franklin complied with an elaborate one that parodied the pompous style of contemporary graveyards. He then reduced it to four of the shortest and best known lines in the American tradition: "Here Skugg / Lies snug / As a bug / In a rug."

Given the brevity of the text, its repetition in the setting is not surprising. In "parlando," separated tones which suggest the staccato chattering of the squirrel, the voice has two statements of "Here Skugg / Lies snug," then finishes the text in a whispered pianissimo seemingly related to his diminuitive size. The piano provides a scampering accompaniment which serves as prelude and interlude but gradually slows to a halt at the end of the one page song in imitation of Skugg's stillness in death.

Example 4.4, measures 10-19. Copyright 1950, G. Schirmer, Inc.; used by permission.

Number three, "Wedlock as old men note," is the first

150

of these texts actually drawn from the almanac, and appeared as the poetic entry for May, 1734. In these compact eight lines, skillfully constructed as to meter and rhyme scheme, Franklin sets forth the cynic's view of marriage, incorporating the familiar warning that "Married in haste, we oft repent at leisure." The final couplet, in a surprise ending, reminds us that the opposite is true, and that even those "married at leisure" may well "repent in haste." Interestingly, in a seeming effort to mitigate these harsh predictions by applying them to unions based on practicality rather than affection, Franklin immediately follows the poem with this adage: "Where there is marriage without love, there will be love without marriage."

Finney has employed his musical craft on the challenging poetic pentameter to recreate the rollicking 6/8 meter of the first song, which alternates the running eighth note scale steps of the motto with dotted half notes held into the next measure as if to slyly underscore a point.

Example 4.5, measures 7-16. Copyright 1950, G. Schirmer, Inc.; used by permission.

Most fittingly for a text written in 1734, the style of the composition is late Baroque counterpoint and indeed the opening lines are set in a canon at the unison, with the upper line of the accompaniment following the voice at the interval of a measure and a half (see Example 4.5). The sevenths and ninths which, in the pianistic introduction, immediately invade the harmony make it clear, however, that this is still the eighteenth century as viewed from the twentieth.

Example 4.6, measures 1-6.   Copyright 1950, G. Schirmer, Inc.; used by permission.

The recurring key contrast, which moves from an opening E major to several measures of C sharp major at the vocal entry (see Examples 4.6 and 4.5), creates a harmonic surprise forecasting the textual one that ends the poem.   As a postlude, Finney cleverly restates the introduction up to the beginning of this modulation, as though to suggest the never-ending circles of human folly.

Example 4.7, measures 54-60.   Copyright 1950, G. Schirmer, Inc.; used by permission.

The text of "Drinking Song," which follows as number four, stems from the 1740's, when Franklin was able to turn from his prospering business to the scientific and mathematical studies which interested him. At this time, he is characterized by Carl Van Doren as "something of a man of pleasure in sober Philadelphia. Comfortable at home, he was convivial in taverns, where he drank rum and Madeira, sang songs, and wrote some."[19] "Fair Venus Calls," Finney's choice, was among these--certainly an admirable example of an eighteenth-century sophisticate's drinking song. In the course of four verses, it praises love, money, and power while recognizing the essential vanity of them all, and predicting an early grave for convivial drinkers in a recurring chorus ("Friends and a bottle still bear the bell"). Notice that the composer makes one of his rare textual changes in this chorus, by omitting the word "still," which scarcely changes the sense of the line, but propels the vocal flow of the 3/2 measure which Finney interpolates into his 4/4 scheme like the sudden, unexpected lurch of a man in his cups.

Example 4.8, measures 55-62. Copyright 1950, G. Schirmer, Inc.; used by permission.

The composer's professed influence in this song by "Hopkinson ... and the eighteenth century ballad songs" is readily seen in the sturdily accented rhythmic patterns, and stolid repeated tones and chordal leaps of the melodic line.

Example 4.9, measures 6-9. Copyright 1950, G. Schirmer, Inc.; used by permission.

The vocal contours, however, are considerably more elaborate than the earlier models (one might, for example, compare Hopkinson's "A Toast" written in honor of George Washington).[20] Further, a brief but arresting modulation from A major to D flat major which lends an invigorating change of harmonic color at the end of verses two and four, is Finney's comment on the drinking party, as an observer from the future.

The cycle having reached its dramatic climax with songs three and four, "When Mars and Venus" offers a reflective change of pace as number five. This rhymed two-line adage appeared in the 1735 edition of Poor Richard. Using the almanac symbols for Mars and Venus, it advised maidens to deny whatever their suitors might ask of them, in a season made astrologically dangerous by the collaboration of the deities of love and warfare. Finney now returns to the thoughtful andante of the opening song, and also employs the 6/8 meter and motto quotations of numbers one and three (see Ex. 4.10). These elements will return again in number seven to complete the cyclical connections. Also notable in this setting are the frequent absences of chordal thirds, which lack creates empty archaic sounding harmonies (see Example 4.10, measures 1 and 2) and the subito pianissimo at the end of the song on the word "deny" which increases the threat in the moralist's mock warning (see Ex. 4.11).

Number 6, "Epitaph on a Talkative Old Maid," uses

Example 4.10, measures 1-5.   Copyright 1950, G. Schirmer,
Inc.; used by permission.

Example 4.11, measures 18-24.   Copyright 1950, G. Schir-
mer, Inc.; used by permission.

the last of the Poor Richard texts.   This one is Franklin's
poetic offering for June, 1738.   In his setting, Finney omits
the word "her" before "cradle" in line three so that a rhyth-
mic suspension may prepare the effect of the descriptive me-
lisma on "talked."

Example 4.12, measures 13-16.   Copyright 1950, G. Schir-
mer, Inc.; used by permission.

This song is made one of the most amusing of the seven by the employment of a Baroque-type perpetual motion figure in the piano which ebbs and flows in dynamics and degree of staccato in imitation of the lady's varied but unending conversational flow.

Example 4.13, measures 9-12. Copyright 1950, G. Schirmer, Inc.; used by permission.

In an artfully contrived ending, Finney has increasing numbers of rests begin to appear in the sixteenth-note groups which also get softer but do not slow down, like a machine that is beginning to fail, but is, nevertheless, loath to stop.

Example 4.14, measures 53-57. Copyright 1950, G. Schirmer, Inc.; used by permission.

The text of "In Praise of Wives," the closing song of the cycle, is another of Franklin's well-made ballads, this one dedicated to his faithful wife Deborah and written in 1742, the twelfth year of their marriage. It was occasioned by a

remark made at "a supper of the Junto or some other con-
vivial club ... that they were all married men and yet sing-
ing the praise of poet's mistresses."[21] The following morn-
ing at breakfast, John Bard, who was one of the better sing-
ers among the club members, received the four verses of
this song, asking him to be ready to perform it at the next
meeting. The quotation of the ballad in the literary sources
indicates a refrain between the verses, beginning "My dear
friends, etc."[22] Finney has omitted this, but otherwise set
the text verbatim, in a style which, as mentioned above, re-
calls the metric and motivic structures of all the odd num-
bers of the cycle.

In the course of the song, Franklin describes his wife
as "my plain country Joan" and insists that virtue is more to
be prized than beauty. One can only speculate as to Mrs.
Franklin's reception of this aspect of his tribute. He does
make it clear, however, that her many sterling qualities have
made her "the joy of (his) life," and Finney matches this with
vocal contours that are the most lyrical and expressive of any
in the set.

Example 4.15, measures 11-16. Copyright 1950, G. Schir-
mer, Inc.; used by permission.

In fact, the high A quoted in the foregoing example is the
highest point of the vocal range of <u>Poor Richard</u>. As this
song, like three and four, is a strophic setting, the timbre
of the cycle's close gains warmth and brilliance through the
four-verse repetition of this phrase.

157

Charles Naginski (1909-1940)
Walt Whitman (1819-1892), Carl Sandburg (1878-1967),
Sara Teasdale (1884-1933)

An item in the New York Times of Sunday, September 8,
1940, reported the performance at Yaddo of a work by Charles
Naginski: "a thirty-one year old composer who was drowned
in Stockbridge Bowl in the Berkshires last month. His sin-
fonietta" it continued, "was performed by [the] chamber or-
chestra under the direction of Richard Donovan as a tribute
to the gifted young composer who came to an untimely end."
Indeed, the musical world had good cause to mourn its loss,
for not since the death of Griffes in 1920 at the age of thirty-
six had so much creative promise been cut off at such an
early stage of its development.

Naginski had been born in Cairo, Egypt, to a Russian
father and a Greek mother. Brought to America as a child,
he studied piano with his father among other teachers, and
having evidenced some talent in composition, was awarded a
fellowship at Juilliard with Rubin Goldmark. Goldmark, who
headed the Juilliard composition department from 1924 til his
death in 1936, was involved in the training of a number of
promising young American composers, among them Copland,
Gershwin, Giannini, Wagenaar, Kagen, and Nordoff. Gold-
mark was the nephew of Karl Goldmark, the Austrian com-
poser, and although Rubin was born in New York City, he
finished the training begun at City College in the country of
his forbears, at the Vienna Conservatory. Never achieving
great reputation himself as a composer, Rubin Goldmark
nevertheless exerted a strong influence on twentieth-century
American composition, and before taking up his prestigious
post at Juilliard, had already left his mark on the southwest
by founding the Colorado College Conservatory in 1894.

Charles Naginski stayed at Juilliard from 1928 to 1933,
the years which spanned the Institute's removal to Claremont
Avenue in 1931. Before the move, it was housed in the old
Vanderbilt mansion on East 52nd Street which offered too few
practice rooms and eventually proved unworkable. An ex-
citing group of students had come together at Juilliard during
the period of Naginski's fellowship. It included Paul Nordoff
and Sergius Kagen as well as a young singer named George
Newton, now retired in Indianapolis from his performing and
teaching career. "Also at the Juilliard then," writes Newton,
"were Celius Dougherty and Vittorio Giannini, but I didn't

158

know them well.... They were older and buried in their work. Charles Naginski I did know fairly well, " he continues. "He spoke five languages including English, all equally badly (I'm told). The Dean thought he needed help so he got us together and we traded lessons in English grammar for accompanying. He was an excellent pianist and it was a good trade for both of us. Nice fellow--tragic end. "[23]

During the thirties, Naginski, like Ross Lee Finney, furthered his compositional studies with Roger Sessions. At the time of his death, he had completed two symphonies, a poem and a suite for orchestra, a ballet called the Minotaur, several works for chamber groups and chamber orchestra, and a number of remarkable songs. What was remarkable about them was not only the innate gifts of arresting harmonic, melodic, and structural invention which they demonstrated. Even more surprising, in a man who was not native born and spoke so many languages, was the depth of his understanding of and response to American poetry, and the force and precision with which he was able to interpret it in musical terms.

Chapter III in the first volume of this series treats Walt Whitman in connection with a Charles Ives setting. Ives may very possibly have been the first American composer to set to music the seemingly problematical verse of Whitman, but many have followed in his footsteps in the course of the twentieth century. One might, in fact, conjecture that Charles Naginski could have become acquainted with the Ives songs when they were first introduced to the public by Aaron Copland at a Yaddo festival in the mid-nineteen thirties. Whether or not this was the initiating course of events, we find Naginski composing two powerful Whitman settings, both of which were published posthumously by G. Schirmer in 1942.[24]

The titles of the songs and the poems were the same: "Look down, fair moon" and "The Ship Starting, " and both poems were included in the collection called Drum Taps which Whitman published in 1865. The decade preceding had been a momentous time for the poet, as it encompassed the first three editions of Leaves of Grass (1855, 1856, 1860) and several years of dedicated service to the wounded soldiers in the field and army hospitals of the Civil War. In an essay called "The Last of the War Cases"[25] Whitman portrays the terrible plight of these men, who were more often dying of starvation or diseases contracted in the hospitals than of their battle-wounds. So great is his compassion for them, and so deep

159

his horror of their fate that one is brought to remember that
Elias Hicks, the fiery dissenting Quaker preacher, had been
a strong influence on the poet's parents and the subject of an
essay by Whitman himself.[26] The truth is that Walt Whit-
man, although drawn to the "inner light" doctrines of the
Quakers, was not a pacifist. He, in fact, believed strongly
in the Union cause, and had begun his hospital visits solely
as a result of seeking out his brother George who had been
reported wounded on the Virginia front.

"Look down, fair moon" is a four-line poetic summary
of the horrors of war, as it exhorts the moonlight, usually
the accompaniment of love scenes, to pour its "nimbus floods"
on the ghastly faces of dead men "on their backs with arms
tossed wide." Naginski's setting is short (two pages) and
structured in a tight, almost ceremonial ABA form which
seems to relate to man's effort to bear the agonies of the
human condition by providing them with an artistic shape.
As a part of this formal emphasis, the composer chooses to
repeat the poem's first line ("Look down, fair moon, and
bathe this scene") at the end of the song, and it might also
be noted that the original poem had read "their arms tossed
wide," while the underlined word was deleted from the 1881
edition. The two A sections of the form--the piano introduc-
tion and postlude--are highly chromatic with clashing poly-
tonal elements in the broken chords. The slow tempo and
very soft, dynamic level of this keyboard dissonance gives
it an ominous and chilling coloristic effect.

Example 4.16, measures 1-3. Copyright 1942, G. Schirmer,
Inc.; used by permission.

In sharp contrast, the B section, which contains the

160

text, is completely diatonic, based on the aeolian mode. This harmonic context, along with the narrow range and repetitions of the vocal line, provide a reference to the Gregorian style which augments the ceremonial aspect of the song suggested above.

Example 4.17, measures 4-6. Copyright 1942, G. Schirmer, Inc.; used by permission.

Set against the liturgical suggestion, however, are the regularly metric, and therefore un-chant-like, hypnotic octaves of the accompaniment's bass line (see measure 6). These prepare a climactic leap of an octave to a mezzo forte outcry: a dramatic moment of protest at the fate of these dead, made the more appalling by its juxtaposition with the appellation "Sacred moon."

Example 4.18, measures 10-12. Copyright 1942, G. Schirmer, Inc.; used by permission.

Notice that the piano introduction concludes with superimposed chords of the tonic and dominant which prepare the vocal entrance in A minor. The second A section, however, takes a different harmonic turn to conclude with a series of diminished chords that trail off into the silence of the unspeakable.

Despite its title, the collection Drum Taps was, from the outset, not limited to war poems. "The Ship Starting" is among those based on other subjects. In the 1881 edition of Leaves of Grass, it was published in the section called "Inscriptions," which had become the title for the opening group of poems. The sea, ships, and journeys over water had long fascinated Whitman, and in these four lines he evokes "the unbounded sea" and the visual splendor of the vessel beginning to move across it with sails and pennant flying. One of the elements that Naginski uses to produce the effect of the ship's initial lumbering and lurching is a cross-rhythmic pattern which is duple in the voice line and triple in the accompaniment:

Example 4.19, measures 1-2. Copyright 1942, G. Schirmer, Inc.; used by permission.

As it begins to "speed so stately," the "emulous waves" are heard in the swooping scales of the piano part (see Ex. 4.20) which are reminiscent of keyboard figures used by Ives in "The Swimmers" (see Volume I, p. 77ff).

Over this instrumental turbulence, the vocal writing remains quite declamatory with much stepwise motion and repetition, either of single notes, or, as in the opening, of the interval of a fifth (see Example 4.19). Also in Example 4.19 may be seen the characteristic accented sevenths and

162

Example 4.20, measure 11. Copyright 1942, G. Schirmer, Inc.; used by permission.

ninths of the accompaniment that imitate the clashing noises of the launching. In this song, Naginski eschews a piano introduction and plunges into the song with the force of sudden movement, but he allows the rolling cascades of scales to continue for several measures at the end, while the vocal line dives into the foaming waters (see Ex. 4.21).

The initial treatment of Carl Sandburg in this series occurs in Chapter 4 of Volume I, where his literary ties to Walt Whitman are discussed. It is also true that there are strong parallels in the life experiences of Whitman and Sandburg. Each had haphazard early schooling, held jobs of all descriptions including manual labor, and engaged primarily in newspaper work to support their early poetic efforts. Even more coincidentally, each was thirty-six years old at the time of his first major publication: Whitman's Leaves of Grass which appeared in 1855, and Sandburg's first group of verse,

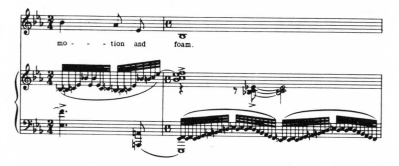

Example 4.21, measures 16-19. Copyright 1942, G. Schir-
mer, Inc.; used by permission.

published in a 1914 issue of Poetry magazine. Two years
later, this group was expanded into the now famous Chicago
Poems, the source of the text for Naginski's only published
Sandburg setting.[27]

"Under the harvest moon" is not typical of the Chicago
Poems in which Carl Sandburg celebrated the world and speech
of the American working man with the attendant coarseness
and ugliness of his twentieth-century environment. Rather,
it seems to be a forerunner of some of the more sensitive
lyrics of Cornhuskers (1918), characterized by one critic as
"delicate perceptions of beauty (in which) raw violence is re-
strained to the point of half-withheld mysticism."[28] The po-
em is in two contrasting stanzas which portray the natural
world's embodiment of life's mysteries: the "soft silver" of
the harvest moon whispering of Death "as a beautiful friend,"
and the "flagrant crimson" of summer roses posing the "un-
answerable questions" of love.

There are two main stresses in each of Sandburg's
lines but the language has a free, speech-like prosodic flow,
against which such highly poetic images as "Death, the gray
mocker," and "the dusk of the wild, red leaves," take on a
heightened intensity. Naginski clothes this poetic rhythm in
flexible, changing vocal patterns which include many triplets
and pairs of sixteenth notes (see "shimmering" in measure
4):

Example 4.22, measures 1-6. Copyright 1940, G. Schirmer, Inc.; used by permission.

The seemingly free flow is unified within an overall 4/4 meter with only one two measure interpolation of 3/2. The latter occurs with Naginski's inspired characterization of Death, which takes the form of a long, mystical cantillation on the piano, sensuously unraveling as the vocal contour dreamily settles on the dominant harmony.

Example 4.23, measures 9-10. Copyright 1940, G. Schirmer, Inc.; used by permission.

This cantillation recurs at the end of the song where it expands by means of strummed piano chords. The expansion is needed to accommodate Sandburg's additional concluding line of verse two--a verbal lingering over the "thousand memories" of love, and their attendant questions.

Example 4.24, measures 21-27. Copyright 1940, G. Schirmer, Inc.; used by permission.

The suggested sound of an exotic folk instrument is implicit in the broken chordal effects and rapid, running passages of the two preceding examples. This atmosphere is deepened by the harmonic and melodic employment of the raised fourth degree of the scale, which is a derivation from the Lydian mode common in Slavic folk song (see the G sharps of Example 4.22). Here, then, is an instance of American art song, originally heavily dependent on British and later German musical models, widening its circle of incoming influences to include Eastern Europe, for further enrichment.

An interesting corollary to this song is an extremely

166

effective setting by Naginski of "Night Song at Amalfi."[29] This poem comes from Sara Teasdale's Riders to the Sea, a collection which she published in 1915, just before her anthology of women's love poetry (see p. 59). In this, probably one of Teasdale's best known lyrics, the poet asks the stars and the sea "what I should give my love" and is answered, to her dismay, by silence. Naginski's musical treatment is triggered by the word "song" in the title, a choice that attests to the manner in which Sara Teasdale usually thought of her poetry, as discussed on page 93. In a flexible rhythmic pattern of varying meters, he creates an improvisatory vocal line whose contours are very similar to the instrumental cantillations quoted above. This melodic construction also draws on the raised Lydian fourth, as well as the augmented second degree of the harmonic minor scale-- an interval which contributes heavily to the poignancy of Eastern European folk music. The piano writing consists of only a few soft, punctuating chords, many of which are bare open fifths. The effect is simply, but brilliantly calculated to suggest a native singer, engaging in a gentle lament to his strummed instrument, the phrases of which fade in and out of a surrounding and threatening "silence."

Sergius Kagen (1908-1964)
Walt Whitman (1819-1892), Carl Sandburg (1878-1967)
Sara Teasdale (1884-1933)

No one in the United States who has been seriously involved with vocal literature during the past fifty years is unfamiliar with the name of Sergius Kagen. Yet, despite his formidable reputation as a coach, accompanist, teacher, and editor, there are relatively few people who know that he was also the composer of a substantial catalog of vocal works, which includes forty-eight songs, three cycles, and two operas.[30]

The Russian Revolution is responsible for the rich contributions of Sergius Kagen to the American musical scene. His father, Isaiah Kagen, was a Lithuanian Jew who had come to the university in St. Petersburg, and remained there as a reporter on and later owner of the Petersburg Leaf. Vera Lipshitz, his mother, was Russian-born, and a brilliant student of languages and literature at the university when she and Kagen met and they married. Isaiah's devoutly Jewish parents never accepted Vera, a self-styled atheist and soon-to-be active member of the Communist Party, but the Kagens prospered financially, and had three sons: Mark, Boris, and Sergius. All were flourishing in the atmosphere of a loving, affluent, intellectual home, complete with summers in a pleasant villa on the River Luga, when the Revolution irrevocably altered the peaceful fabric of their lives. Mark, the eldest son, who had been a promising young pianist, was killed in 1917 fighting the White Russians, and Vera, who perhaps blamed his death on her own political involvement, did not leave her room for an entire year. Onto Sergius' nine-year-old shoulders now fell the task of trying to replace his talented older brother and, his parents having enrolled him in the Petersburg Conservatory under Glazunov's personal supervision, he undertook it with great energy.

The famine and destruction attendant on the Revolution decimated the Petersburg population and two of Sergius' aunts together with their families did not survive the cataclysm. By 1920, the Isaiah Kagens were forced to seek an uncertain sanctuary in Berlin, which they reached with great hardship after traveling for several months in cattle cars. Sergius, still only twelve, had already experienced an emotional and historical lifetime. He emerged from it, and from his mother's intellectual fostering, with a drive toward artistic excellence and the capacity to endure the discomfort of unrelenting hard work. Another formative influence had been Vera's fears and superstitions which had caused the boy while still in Russia to be educated at home under a "nanny's" supervision. Sergius developed, as a result of the isolation, a somewhat shy and retiring personality which precluded easy intimacy, but at the same time were planted the seeds of stubborn, independent thinking. Later they would blossom into a remarkable career.

In Berlin, Sergius enrolled at the Hochschule für Musik to study piano with Leonid Kreutzer, while his father became a partner in a loan corporation. The business failed to prosper in an economy still weak from the effects of World War I, and increasingly hostile to both Jews and Russians. By 1922, the Isaiah Kagens began to emigrate, one at a time, to the United States, leaving the fifteen-year-old Sergius alone in Germany for a period of time. Finally settled in New York City, the young man undertook a routine of keeping house for his working parents, and practicing the piano, but even in that musical center found no one who drew him as a teacher until he heard the playing of Carl Friedberg, [31] in the late twenties. Friedberg taught at Juilliard, which was heavily endowed and therefore free to those passing the entrance examinations. In an audition now become legendary, Kagen began to play through the entire 48 preludes and fugues of Bach's Well Tempered Clavier, and was accepted when his intention and ability to execute it became clear to the judges.

Kagen's experience as a Juilliard student during the years 1930-1934 was, like all of his previous life to that point, a mixture of trauma and inspiration. The centrally important relationship with Carl Friedberg, his teacher, proceeded well on a personal level, but proved musically disappointing. Kagen, whose technique had been largely self-taught according to the traditions of the Petersburg Conservatory through Leschetizsky, had difficulty assimilating the technical instructions of his teacher. This was because Friedberg himself did not play as he taught, but based his extraordinary pianistic communication on the ability to form a clear mental image of the composition and on a total intellectual grasp of the score, which enabled the free operation of musical instinct in performance.[32] These principles later became cornerstones of Kagen's own teaching but while he was in the process of formulating them, he was sufficiently discouraged by the problems with his professor, and by his lack of perfect pitch among a group of students who mostly possessed it, to contemplate abandoning music as a career.

Kagen's highly developed critical faculties and independent thinking led him, in fact, to a clash with Frank Damrosch in a conducting class, which was nearly disastrous. Damrosch was the director of the Institute, and expelled Kagen after a heated exchange of insults in German, whereupon Carl Friedberg arranged for him to be admitted to the Juilliard Graduate School to complete his diploma in piano. Over and against these struggles, however, were the two very rewarding experiences of the composer's student days. One was friendship with fellow students, and among the most important of these friends was Charles Naginski, foreign-born like himself, and struggling to gain a foothold in American music. Naginski was the witness at his wedding to Genevieve Greer in 1937, and one can well imagine the depth of Kagen's grief at the loss of his young friend just three years later.

The other great light, which not only illuminated Kagen's life as a student but determined the direction of his unique career and contributions to music, was Marcella Sembrich, the brilliant recital and opera singer who was 74 at the time of their meeting. At the suggestion of Naginski, who could not work with her, Kagen tried out, successfully, as an accompanist for her Juilliard students, and the two worked closely together until her death in 1935. Their European backgrounds gave them a common experience and Sembrich could speak to the young man both in German and in her native Polish which was enough like Russian for him to understand it. Marcella Sembrich became probably his most important teacher and from her he learned the vocal literature and how it should be performed. At her death, he became the purveyor of the rich tradition, and the career of Sergius Kagen as professional accompanist, coach, and teacher began to flourish. Genevieve Greer, who became Mrs. Kagen, 33 had been a Sembrich student, and many of her other students whom Kagen had accompanied in her New York studio and Lake George summer home, continued working with him at her passing. Several were Metropolitan Opera stars, and there was scarcely a well known singer in the thirties and forties whom Kagen did not accompany in Town Hall recitals or on short tours out of New York.

His teaching connections with Juilliard grew from parttime to full faculty status in 1940 and his areas of pedagogy continued to increase. Beginning as a vocal coach and instructor of a lieder class for singers, he eventually became a member of the voice faculty and also developed a training program for accompanists, 34 which has since been emulated by a number of graduate music departments around the country. John Hanks, professor of voice at Duke University (see p. 51), was profoundly influenced by Sergius Kagen's vocal literature classes at Juilliard, of which he was a member both before and after his service in World War II (1941 and 1946). 35 These highly organized, demanding classes for which each student had to prepare five or six songs twice a week, became the model for a similar course at Duke in the middle sixties in which the writer participated as accompanist and teacher of student accompanists. Professor Hanks remembers Kagen as a man who spoke English with a slight accent, and, in the European fashion, was impersonal and rarely complimentary in class. His criticisms of the performances included matters vocal and interpretative. Always, he stressed communication of the text, and his command of European languages was of great help in training these American singers to be expressive in the foreign bodies of literature.

By the end of the forties, Kagen began assembling in book form the gleanings of his fantastically wide experience

as teacher and performer. In close succession, he published
Music for the Voice, [36] his descriptive list of concert and
teaching material; On Studying Singing, [37] a distillation of his
basic philosophy which he planned for many years and wrote
in three weeks; and the opening collections in the International
Publishing Company's series of song and aria editions which
would eventually number thirty-nine volumes. His life as a
performer was still active, and from 1940 to 1950, he was a
member and unofficial director of the original Bach Aria
Group, whose singers were drawn from his students. The
fifties also saw a memorable recital collaboration with the
American baritone, Mack Harrell, [38] who was a colleague of
Kagen's on the Juilliard faculty, as well as the writing of
many articles for the Juilliard Review. All of this frenetic,
"in season" activity, was counterbalanced by soul-restoring
summers in Vermont, where the Kagens rented peaceful but
spartan quarters for many years. Money was always tight,
for the brilliant musician was an indifferent businessman, and
depended on his wife to manage most of the affairs of daily
living, including driving the family car. For the last four
years of his life, Sergius Kagen finally owned a summer home
with some of the creature comforts such as electricity and a
screened porch. The couple planned to retire there, but in
March, 1964, Kagen woke with a scream seemingly from one
of the occasional nightmares which had plagued him all his
life. In reality, it was the final episode of a heart condition
he had had for a number of years. His labors at an end,
Kagen was buried in his beloved Vermont.

In an article titled "The American Concert Song, "
Sergius Kagen expressed in 1954 his long-held conviction that
"the concert song is a stepchild of contemporary American
music. "[39] He deplored the dearth of "musically fine songs
in English" which could serve as models for young compos-
ers, and categorized the available, but undesirable American
songs as either light-weight "salon" types in the Chaminade
style, or "wild" songs with tormented and unsingable vocal
lines. [40] According to Professor Hanks (see p. 170), Kagen's
vocal literature classes in the forties indeed contained no
American songs, as though he considered none worthy of at-
tention. Interestingly, however, at the end of the 1954 arti-
cle Kagen expressed his optimism about the future "for in the
last few years, " he stated, "a number of startlingly good
songs has appeared in America. "[41] In 1949, in response to
his wife's challenge, Sergius Kagen had begun to write his
own songs, and this, the most creative of all his varied en-
terprises, brought him the greatest satisfaction during the
last fifteen years of his life.

171

After having played all the finest songs of the Western vocal tradition in superlative fashion for two decades, Kagen's aim in starting to compose his own was twofold. He wanted to help develop a literature of "serious" but vocally grateful songs in English, and he also wanted to be among those involved in creating a recognizably American style in the art song. Like many of the foreign-born, Sergius Kagen had deep emotional ties to the adopted country which had tried and tested, but also nurtured him. His wife, Genevieve, had been born in Davis, Oklahoma, and her family background was partly American Indian: a heritage as close to the ethnic roots of the New World as it was possible to come. Kagen was drawn to this, and to the literary heritage of America as well. Almost seventy-five percent of his songs are based on American texts, and they are, for the most part, settings of poems which he had known well and loved for a good many years. They include the works of a healthy cross section of American poetry, ranging from Whitman and Dickinson in the nineteenth century, through Sandburg, Teasdale, cummings, and MacLeish, to Langston Hughes and James Agee, his close contemporaries in the twentieth century. The poems that he chose for setting, with the exception of the Three Satires cycle, were for the most part somber, reflective, or dramatic in tone. Kagen, in his rejection of the "salon" style which he also characterized as "encore" songs, was clearly determined to avoid the frivolous in his own work. Another overall aspect of his song-writing is interesting to observe at the outset. In direct contrast to the songs of John Duke which frequently display an elaborate pianism, Sergius Kagen's place all emphasis on the text and vocal line. The man who spent his life giving inconspicuous but invaluable support to singers continued this position in writing accompaniments which are sparse enough to highlight the voice, but which unfailingly outline the singer's notes.

The five settings of Whitman, Sandburg, and Teasdale about to be discussed, were all written during the flood-tide years of 1949 and 1950 which produced a total of 41 songs. The Whitman fragment, "I Think I Could Turn...."[42] is the only instance of Kagen setting this poet, and the lines are taken from "Song of Myself," the central poem of Leaves of Grass.[43] In them, Whitman turns from his celebration of himself and his fellow men to extol the virtues of animals who, "placid and self-contained ... do not whine about their condition (nor) weep for their sins, " and are nowhere "respectable or unhappy over the whole earth." The poet continues to marvel that "not one is demented with the mania

172

of owning things" nor do they "make me sick discussing their
duty to God." It is easy to see why these iconoclastic senti-
ments, striking at America's prevailing materialism and pi-
etism, would have had great appeal to Kagen whose family
had suffered much from humanity's religious and political de-
votions, and who had chosen a life of artistic excellence over
financial comfort.

The setting is a prime example of the careful prosody
which characterizes all of the composer's word-setting. The
vocal line is declamatory, with many repeated notes, and a
flexible use of meter and rhythms within measures to con-
form to Whitman's free flow of American speech patterns.

Example 4.25, measures 15-17. Copyright 1952, Mercury
Music Corp.; used by permission.

The song is unified by a tonal, but chromatic walking bass
pattern which seems to suggest the measured placidity of the
animal world and which is repeated at different pitch levels.
These sequences take on a rising curve as the fortissimo cli-
max expresses the madness of those obsessed by possessions
(see Example 4.25). Kagen repeats the opening two lines of
the poem to create an ABA form and as the vocal line returns

from storming protest to philosophic musing, the walking bass trails off on a scalar descent in the Phrygian mode, but stops a frustrated half step from musical and emotional completion.

Example 4.26, measures 26-30. Copyright 1952, Mercury Music Corp.; used by permission.

Kagen's harmonic style throughout his song catalog which is heavily chromatic, often atonal, and at times serial, indicates that he was in touch with twentieth-century trends of the musical avant-garde that had grown out of Richard Strauss and Scriabin toward Schoenberg and his school. He was equally aware of developments in contemporary poetry, and became an early fan of Carl Sandburg. The poet's "plain speech" and sympathy for the common man touched a responsive chord in this highly cultivated musician whose life had been ruled by economic and historic forces beyond his control. "Mag"[44] is a moving dramatic monologue from Sandburg's Chicago Poems: the lament of a man who has been brought, by the grinding daily struggle of poverty, to wish that he had never married, and that "the kids had never come." The desperate outpouring is powerfully set by Kagen in a series of rising waves, with vocal contours that arch over every "wish" and settle back in discouragement on the minor triads of E flat, B flat and F sharp.

174

Example 4.27, measures 1-8. Copyright 1950, Weintraub
Music Co.; used by permission.

The portrayal of the speaker's mental anguish is intensified
by the clashing, polytonal underpinning of an ostinato figure
in the pianist's left hand, which begins as octaves (see Ex-
ample 4.27) but changes to dissonant major sevenths behind
his peaks of desperation.

Example 4.28, measures 25-28. Copyright 1950, Weintraub
Music Co.; used by permission.

Sandburg ends the poem with his litany-like refrain,
"I wish to God I never saw you, Mag. / I wish to God the
kids had never come." Kagen lets this die away dynamically
as though through the speaker's exhaustion, but saves a com-
plex of clashing seconds and ninths in the accompaniment and
a vocal leap of an augmented fourth for the final measures.
The effect is that of a mind tormented beyond further protest
or endurance, and trying to slip into oblivion.

Example 4.29, measures 36-39. Copyright 1950, Weintraub
Music Co.; used by permission.

Sandburg's Chicago Poems had been the occasion of
critical derision at their publication in 1916. By the appear-
ance of the Good Morning, America collection in 1928, Carl
Sandburg had been accepted into the mainstream of American
literature, and indeed its title poem was read at a Harvard
Phi Beta Kappa investiture. Kagen's setting of "Maybe"[45]
from this collection, is his shortest song (one page) and a
contrast in every way to "Mag." This poem is also a mono-
logue, but the speaker here is a young girl, rather coyly

176

speculating on whether or not her suitor will propose, and
what her answer will be. This is a totally diatonic setting
without a single chromatic alteration. The resulting modal
melodic structures lend an Elizabethian/Appalachian flavor of
ancient innocence to the song, as do the "Scotch-snap" rhyth-
mic figures (sixteenth followed by dotted eighth), which inten-
sify the suggestion of British folk origins.

Example 4.30, measures 1-5.   Copyright 1950, Weintraub
Music Co.; used by permission.

     The accompaniment, however, employs soft dissonant
intervals and superimposed chordal elements to establish the
twentieth century, and the uncertainty of the speaker's ma-
nipulative state of mind (see Example 4.30).   Meter changes
are again characteristically frequent, and the vocal line moves
in appropriately melting, legato dotted note and triplet rhyth-
mic patterns.   A lone measure of pianistic melody echoes
and telescopes the preceding vocal phrase and seems, by its
poignant pleading, to prepare the decision to "say yes."

177

Example 4.31, measures 10-18. Copyright 1950, Weintraub Music Co.; used by permission.

The two poems by Sara Teasdale that Kagen chose for setting stem from an inner environment of delicate perceptions that is a far cry from Whitman's and Sandburg's world of strong, primary colors and basic, everyday reality. Both of the poems, however, are founded in regret, and the certain knowledge of the impermanence of natural beauty and human emotion. Interestingly, "A June Day"[46] is a setting of a short lyric from the collection Stars Tonite of 1930 which was subtitled Verses for Boys and Girls (see p. 94). The poem is, basically, an exquisite verbal description of the sights and sounds "Down where the river sleeps in the reeds," during the passage from morning to "blue night" of an early summer day. The only jarring note in this peace and beauty occurs in the final couplet where "the day was ended / That never will come again," and it is worthy of note that Teasdale does not spare her young audience this disquieting thought.

Kagen's setting takes off from the opening line, "I heard a red-winged blackbird singing," and creates a background of pianistic bird-song that weaves in and out behind the voice and also provides the instrumental introduction and postlude.

Example 4.32, measures 1-5. Copyright 1950, Weintraub Music Co.; used by permission.

178

The high tessitura of the vocal line and accompaniment (all above middle C) approach the vibratory range of the black-bird's singing while the rapid rhythmic patterns in short, disjointed, often leaping groups of notes, suggest his darting and hopping.

Example 4.33, measures 16-19. Copyright 1950, Weintraub Music Co.; used by permission.

A lyrical melodic curve descends with the fall of "blue night, "

Example 4.34, measures 30-33. Copyright 1950, Weintraub Music Co.; used by permission.

and the returning bird-song of the postlude consigns the day to memory. All of the foregoing is saved from triteness or banality by Kagen's harmonic skill in manipulating the poly-tonality which pervades this setting. For the most part, the left hand of the accompaniment and the vocal line derive from the same chordal formations, while the right hand superim-poses highly clashing structures often a minor ninth apart (see measure one). The result is a suspended, objective, and universal quality in the setting which throws the lush

179

images of Teasdale's poem into sharp relief, as the more romantic treatments often afforded her poetry frequently fail to do.

"Let It Be Forgotten"[47] sets another eight-line poem, this time from Teasdale's Flame and Shadow, a collection published in 1920, at the height of her popularity. In this gently enigmatic lyric, the poet never states just what is to be forgotten "as a fire that once was singing gold." One can easily imagine, however, that with the passage of six years since the beginning of her disappointing marriage, Teasdale had long given up her early dream of a fulfilling love relationship. In one of her most telling lines, which ends verse one, she in fact states the credo of her remaining years: "Time is a kind friend, he will make us old."

The apparent simplicity of Kagen's setting of this poetry is the source of its artistic force. The dynamic level is mostly quiet, and the voice line moves over a fairly narrow range in quasi-recitative fashion as the piano strikes soft, intermittent chords. Kagen's command of his free-flowing prosody suggests an intimate acquaintance with Monteverdi, for he has succeeded in adapting the expressive plasticity of the "stile recitativo" to the aesthetic climate of the mid-twentieth century. Quartal[48] harmonies are prevalent in the chordal constructions and their empty ambivalence supports the poet's withdrawal of psychic energy.

Example 4.35, measures 1-4. Copyright 1950, Weintraub Music Co.; used by permission.

The end of the song decreases the movement of the already slow tempo by augmenting the length of the vocal notes, as the half-note triplet on "hushed foot-fall" almost drags to a halt.

hushed foot-fall __ In a long - for - got - ten snow. __

Example 4.36, measures 23-27. Copyright 1950, Weintraub
Music Co.; used by permission.

The three final bi-tonal piano chords unify the song as they
recall the opening sequence at a lower pitch, and their wispy
evanescence seems to complete the process of forgetting.

Paul Nordoff (1909-1977)
Conrad Aiken (1889-1973), Elinor Wylie (1885-1928)

Paul Nordoff was born in Philadelphia and was largely raised
by his grandmother who was from upstate Pennsylvania. One
of his strongest childhood memories was of her standing at
the foot of his bed and reciting poetry to him before saying
goodnight.[49] Poetry, then, was an early and familiar friend,
and, as a consequence, the medium of song became a highly
congenial one to the composer.

Nordoff, whose musical talents were developing rapidly,
entered the Philadelphia Conservatory of Music at the age of
fourteen to study piano with Olga Samaroff, the great Ameri-
can pianist and teacher who had been born under the name of
Hickenlooper in San Antonio, Texas. In 1929, Nordoff joined
Charles Naginski as a fellowship student in composition of
Rubin Goldmark's at Juilliard, having been brought to Gold-
mark's attention on the strength of his settings of German
and French poetry. George Newton (see p. 158) remembers
Nordoff as well as Naginski and Kagen, and recalls that he
"tried to get him to write some music that a basso could
sing." Apparently, Paul Nordoff's talents as a song com-
poser had already been recognized by faculty and fellow stu-
dents alike.

181

In 1932, Nordoff completed his Master of Music de-
gree at Juilliard and on the basis of Guggenheim fellowships
awarded him in 1933 and 1935, was able to travel and com-
pose in Europe. Germany seemed an initially hospitable en-
vironment. He concertized with a Munich singer and became
friendly with the last grand Duke of Hesse. By 1937, how-
ever, with Hitler's political ambitions becoming ominously
clear, Nordoff left Germany, after arranging for the publica-
tion of twelve of his songs by Schott and Company. Back in
America, he was appointed, at the age of twenty-nine, to
head the composition department of the Philadelphia Conser-
vatory, where fifteen years earlier he had entered as an as-
piring student. Nordoff held this position for five years and
resigned in 1943. The year 1945 saw him entering the world
of university music as assistant professor at Michigan State
College; it was also the year of his marriage to Sabina Zay,
a union which produced three children. [50] His second and last
university-level appointment was as professor of music at
Bard College, a small, well-endowed liberal arts school at
Annandale-on-Hudson, and he served in this capacity from
1948 to 1959. No doubt on sabbatical from the college, he
was one of the first composers to take advantage of the Mac-
Dowell Colony's new winter facilities, and his residence there
of several months was reported by the Musical Courier of
January 15, 1956.

The rise of Nordoff's teaching career was paralleled
by his growing reputation as a composer. During the forties
and fifties, he was commissioned to write ballets for both
Martha Graham and Agnes de Mille, an opera for Columbia
University, and orchestral works for the Louisville and New
Orleans symphonies. [51] There were also several chamber
works composed during this period, as well as some piano
pieces and a large number of songs. But paralleling Nor-
doff's success as a conventional composer in those years
was his growing interest in the spiritual teachings of Ru-
dolph Steiner's Anthroposophy, [52] and their practical appli-
cations to the education of handicapped children. Having
been led further in this direction by information concerning
the central nervous system's strong response to music in
children with cerebral palsy, Paul Nordoff enrolled in the
Combs College of Music in Philadelphia, and in 1960 emerged
with a Bachelor's degree in Music Therapy, and a new life.
The years which remained to him were spent working with
severely handicapped children in many institutions in the
United States and Europe. Together with his collaborator,
Clive Robbins, he wrote a number of articles and books de-

scribing the work,[53] as well as several musical plays and many play-songs designed for use in the therapeutic situation.[54]

Nordoff's drastic change of his musical focus evoked very mixed reactions from his friends and artistic colleagues. e.e. cummings, with whom he had had a close relationship for fifteen years and who adored the Nordoff settings of his poetry,[55] never came to understand the seeming desertion. On the other hand, Mrs. Nellie Lee (Curtis) Bok,[56] who was, in mid-century, a leading Philadelphia patron of the arts, described her longtime friend as a self-sacrificing and saintly man[57] and opened her home to him whenever he returned to Philadelphia. It was on such an occasion (February 5, 1975)[58] that the author had the privilege of meeting Paul Nordoff, who was at that time under treatment at the University of Pennsylvania Hospital for the malignancy which took his life two years later. The interior of the narrow, red-brick Philadelphia townhouse was dark with faded opulence and the composer a gaunt shadow of the person shown in earlier photographs, but he spoke of song-writing with great warmth and played his own on an ancient, mellow Steinway. In studying many songs, Nordoff said, he had realized that "a composer tells you something about himself when he chooses a poem; he says 'this means something to me.' Debussy's (choices) tell us much about his humour and loneliness and great spirit." He went on to observe that he had continued to write songs all his life (two more e.e. cummings settings were completed even during his years as a therapist) despite the fact that "publishers ignore them because they don't sell. They should publish them anyway," said Nordoff, with heated emphasis.

The composer's expressed frustration was easy to understand. Of the dozens of Nordoff songs listed in his ASCAP catalog, only twenty, plus the ten of Anthony's Song Book (see note 50), have ever been published. A recent effort in England to bring a number of the e.e. cummings settings to publication seems as yet unfruitful. Of the published songs, three are to texts by Conrad Aiken, whose early poetry, suffused as it was with verbal musical images, seemed to evoke the desire in the young composer to clothe it in actual music.

The life of Conrad Aiken was a strange mixture of conservative academic and literary events set over against bizarre personal incident. He was born in Savannah to parents who were transplanted New Englanders: a brilliant physician father, and an attractive mother who was the daughter of a

Massachusetts Congregational Minister. Conrad was the eldest of three sons and his mother's favorite. One can well imagine the effect on the boy, then eleven-and-a-half years old, of discovering his parents dead after the father had committed murder followed by suicide. The two younger brothers having been adopted by a Philadelphia family, Conrad now reclaimed his New England heritage and went to live with a great, great aunt in New Bedford, Massachusetts.

In 1907, he entered Harvard with an illustrious class which included Heywood Broun, Walter Lippmann, and John Reed. Having discovered his literary talents when he composed a poem at nine, Aiken now developed them with extensive contributions to the Harvard Advocate and Monthly. Placed on probation during his senior year for cutting classes to complete a poetic undertaking, Aiken resigned in protest, spent six months traveling in Europe, and returned to complete his Harvard degree in 1912. A few days after graduation, he married Jessie McDonald who, as the first of the poet's three wives, would also become the mother of his three children.

Conrad Aiken, throughout his career, had what is only dreamt of by most men of literature--a small independent income that made it possible for him to develop a richly varied career without the usual strains of financial necessity. Poetry was his earliest medium and one to which he would return throughout his life. In 1914, just as America's poetic renaissance was dawning, he published Earth Triumphant, and by 1920, there were five more collections of his verse in print. Briefly attracted to the Imagist movement, he moved, in 1915, from Cambridge to Boston to be near John Gould Fletcher, and for the next half-dozen years developed acquaintanceships with Pound, Eliot, Lowell, and others involved in the "new" poetry. In 1922, he took his family for a three-year stay in England and returned there in the thirties with his third wife, Mary Hoover (an artist), to conduct the Jeake's House Summer School for a small number of writers and painters. World War II forced the removal of this school to South Dennis, Cape Cod. Ironically, the second major war of the century had caught up with the man who had been exempted from service in the first on the grounds of his claim that poetry was "an essential industry."

Other than the summer school, Aiken's only formal teaching position was a year spent as an English instructor at Harvard in 1927-28. This left his energies free to be invested in the many volumes of poetry and fiction he produced, as well as in extensive activities as editor and critic. From 1916 to 1919, he was a contributing editor to The Dial; during the twenties and thirties, he served as American or London correspondent to various periodicals on either side of the Atlantic; and between all of his own writing tasks, he found time to edit anthologies of American and English poetry. Although critical approbation was a long time coming to Conrad Aiken, by the age of sixty the literary world had begun to recognize his considerable achievements. He served as Consultant in Poetry to the Library of Congress from 1950 to 1952, and during the following two decades received many awards, such as the Bollingen Prize (1956), Academy of American Poets Fellowship (1957), and National Medal for Literature (1969).

From our present vantage point, it becomes easy to see that Conrad Aiken's early neglect was largely due to the initially overshadowing reputations of his contemporaries such as Ezra Pound and T. S. Eliot, and to the fact that he "refused to yield to the temptation to become fashionable."[59] Extraordinarily gifted as to the technique of his craft, Aiken also brought a deep interest in psychoanalytical theory (likely stemming from his childhood trauma) to bear on the poetic writings with the result that "no one has so exhaustively ... explored the problems of the modern consciousness."[60] However, in the early poetry, from which the Nordoff settings are drawn, Aiken was still involved in the attempt to "formulate independent modes and philosophies."[61] Since childhood, he had been "passionately fond of music,"[62] and at thirteen had come under the influence of Edgar Allan Poe, a poet whose obsession with the "music" of words is discussed in Volume I of this series.[63] It is not surprising then, that Conrad Aiken should attempt to infuse many parallels from the art of music--its forms, thematic structures, rhythmic patterns and tone-colors--into the poetic language and constructions of his early collections. He made his intentions clear by the inclusion of such words as "nocturne," "symphony" and "prelude" in his poetic titles, and suggested further musical allusions by the use of sectional repetition and a heavy reliance on mnemonic values.

In 1942, Paul Nordoff published "White Nocturne,"[64] one of his finest songs, to a poetic text from Aiken's volume called Nocturne of Remembered Spring and Other Poems (1917). The title of the poem indicates the writer's intention to combine the musical suggestion of a subdued, melancholy "night-piece" and visual, coloristic elements with his verbal material. The color effects, all overwhelmingly "white, " are created by images of falling snow, pale hands, and the petals of white flowers, while the subdued tone of melancholy derives from the dramatic portrait which unfolds of a man and woman saddened by their knowledge of change and time passing. Nordoff has actually set only the twelve lines of section four, out of a poem which in its entirety runs to six sections and 143 lines. By this choice, he achieved a text which was the perfect length for a song, and which became a brief lyric expressing the memory of an exquisite moment, without the "sense of terror, and of death"[65] that is always strong in Aiken and that pervades the rest of the poem.

Section four, which begins "I would like to touch this snow with the wind of a dream, " is, like the rest of "White Nocturne, " made up of five-stress lines which employ varying rhyme schemes occasionally and inconsistently. In the original printing, line two read "With a sudden warmth of music and turn it all" but by the time it was reprinted in collections, Aiken had shortened it to "And turn it all. " Nordoff went farther with the tightening process, omitting "that" in line three, and "floating in water" in line five. Now with a text shaped to his design, the composer was faced with the problem of finding a musical style appropriate to this very sensuous verse, which already possessed "a subaqueous music, strangely like the magic of Debussy. "[66] It may indeed have been this very quality in the poetry which attracted Nordoff, who had always been a great admirer of French song in general and Debussy in particular. For his setting, then, he drew heavily on the hazy world of Impressionistic harmony, and placed an exquisitely contoured, delicate vocal line against a wash of parallel fifths, octaves, and non-resolving cluster chords.

I would like to   touch   this   snow____ with the wind of a

dream,___ And turn it all to pet - als of ros - es.

Example 4.37, measures 4-10.   Copyright 1942, Oliver Ditson Co.; used by permission.

The formal structure is simply but perfectly adapted to the text. It repeats the music of Example 4.37 behind the two poetic repetitions of "I would like to touch this snow," etc., but increases the dynamic level each time to accommodate to the emotion suggested by the changing second line of each couplet.

night.   I, I would like to touch this snow___

___ with the wind of a dream: ___ And hear you sing - ing a -

187

Example 4.38, measures 34-44.   Copyright 1942, Oliver Ditson Co.; used by permission.

The effect is of a gradually gathering crescendo of longing, which the poet, lacking the greater variety of musical device, had attempted to suggest by altering the punctuation marks that follow repetitions of the refrain:

    a) I would like to touch this snow with the wind of a dream,
    b) I would like to touch this snow with the wind of a dream;
    c) I would like to touch this snow with the wind of a dream:

Also woven into the form is a recurrent rhythmic figure of a tied over half note followed by three eighths which first appears in the piano introduction

Example 4.39, measures 1-3.   Copyright 1942, Oliver Ditson Co.; used by permission.

and undergoes metamorphosis and expansion into a full-blown instrumental counterpoint.

Example 4.40, measures 11-13. Copyright 1942, Oliver Ditson Co.; used by permission.

There is only one instance of word-painting in this setting which for the most part is designed to suggest the atmosphere of the text rather than specific images: the section which deals with walking "through snow" and "among the hills immortally white" pulls into a regular 3/4 rhythm and a piu mosso tempo, suggesting a measured and purposeful stride. The harmonic mode also becomes major at this point, but soon begins to lose its accidentals and fade back to the softness of the minor for the setting of "Golden by noon and blue by night." Notice also in Example 4.38 that the major/minor ambiguity which characterizes the three repeated phrases becomes even more dreamlike and inconclusive with the descent of the brief postlude's pianistic melody to the lowered (Phrygian) second step of the E tonality (measures 43-44).

Nordoff's two other Aiken settings both appeared in the Schott publications of 1938, which were originally issued through the Mainz office and later reprinted many times by Schott and Co. in London. "Music I heard with you"[67] sets one of Aiken's best known poems, which had originally been published in Turns and Movies (1917), his third collection of verse. As the first of a group titled "Discordants," this poem establishes the tone of the rest, in its lament over the loss of love and of its power to transfigure the physical world ("bread I broke with you was more than bread"). In this lyric, one can observe many of the poet's literary preoccupations: not only the threat of time, but the images of hands, fingers, and of course, music, begin to be seen as typical of this period. Nordoff's writing also relates to the later "White Nocturne" which it prefigures, in the use of a recurrent pianistic pattern, this time a rising and falling curve of eighth notes in the left hand.

189

Example 4.41, measures 1-5. Copyright 1938, Schott and Co.; used by permission.

In all other respects, however, this is a very different setting from "White Nocturne," and the arching eighth notes release floods of pain, in a world of color and sensation far removed from the other's dreamy pallor.

Nordoff makes no changes at all in this poem and adapts Aiken's pentameter (a favorite poetic meter in his early work) to an unbroken 4/4 musical meter by setting one or two words in each line to a longer note value, such as a dotted quarter (see Example 4.41). Harmony is once again a prime ally of the composer's, and one of the most poignant musical moments of the setting occurs with the placing of a soft pianistic appoggiatura over the voice's F sharp on the word "dead." This is immediately followed by an unexpected sequential repetition which begins to pull toward a wistful G major and the memory of the beloved touch on familiar objects (see Ex. 4.42).

In 1922, Aiken published Priapus and the Pool, a collection of twenty-five lyrics, several of which have been called "as skillful as those of any contemporary American singer."[68]

190

Example 4.42, measures 8-13.   Copyright 1938, Schott and
Co.; used by permission.

One of these is titled "This is the shape of the leaf," and
it contains six masterfully constructed verses with an intri-
cate metric scheme and mellifluous flow of language that are
reminiscent of Swinburne in an earlier century.   The tree on
which the "leaf" grows is "In a land we never shall see":
seemingly a mystical paradise inhabited in the evening by
"three beautiful pilgrims" who wait for a bird's "clear phrase
in the twilight / To fill the blue bell of the world."   From
the hindsight of familiarity with Nordoff's attraction in later
years to the spiritual worlds described in Rudolph Steiner's
Anthroposophy, the young composer's identification with this
poem is readily understandable.   His setting[69] is atypical
but extremely interesting, its salient feature being a narrow-
range, chant-like vocal line, frequently doubled by the piano
at the interval of a fifth (see Ex. 4.43).   The meditative, hypnot-
ic effect of this circular motion is heightened by the Gregorian
suggestion of the empty fifths, and the flexible meter which al-
ternates between 6/4 and 4/4.   In an inspired gesture, Nordoff
provides contrast to the step-wise motion with his setting of
the moment when the silence is ended by the bird's singing.
Here the vocal line introduces the excitement of leaping in-
tervals up to an octave, while the piano plays superimposed

Example 4.43, measures 1-4.   Copyright 1938, Schott and
Co.; used by permission.

chords whose sonorities continue to increase as the song of
the bird gradually fills "the blue bell of the world."

Example 4.44, measures 27-32.   Copyright 1938, Schott and
Co.; used by permission.

The other settings in Nordoff's 1938 Schott publications derive from a mixture of English and American poetic texts. One of these is Elinor Wylie's "Fair Annette's Song,"[70] which was set by Mary Howe some twenty years later (see page 20). The poem, in eight lines beginning "One thing comes and another thing goes," creates the atmosphere of a folk song by the simplicity of the language and universality of the recorded experience ("It is sad to remember and sorrowful to pray"). Mary Howe's setting embedded this text in jewel-like fashion within a harmonically and pianistically sophisticated accompaniment, and contributed a vocal line equally elaborate in its rhythmic variation, leaping contour, and extended range. The effect of this is to expose the intricate psychological levels which underly the apparent simplicity of the statements.

Nordoff's setting takes the opposite course. His song, which is two pages long instead of Howe's five, completely avoids instrumental or vocal elaboration. With a diatonic voice line that is all stepwise motion and chordal leaps, he emphasizes the innocent grace of the poetry,

Example 4.45, measures 1-2. Copyright 1938, Schott and Co.; used by permission.

and by turning from F major to the Aeolian mode of this tonal center, he lends a late-medieval atmosphere to the Ophelia-like poignancy of the words (see Ex. 4.46). Notice the added measure of 6/4 in Example 4.46. This is the only change in the otherwise strophic treatment of the second four-line verse, and its rhythmic extension and crescendo followed by a subito piano suggest "Fair Annette's" suppressed dismay over the fleeting loveliness of spring.

A final point of interest in Example 4.46 is the capital "M" on the word "May" which occurs in the Nordoff set-

193

Example 4.46, measures 12-16. Copyright 1938, Schott and Co.; used by permission.

ting. In Wylie's poem, the "m" is lower case, and the writer is clearly employing the word to mean "hawthorne," according to the British usage. Mary Howe's setting adheres to the lower case, leaving us to wonder whether Nordoff's embodies his own misconception, or a printer's error.

NOTES

1. The reader will notice that, with the exceptions of Walt Whitman and Emily Dickinson, whose work paved the way for the American "poetic renaissance," Benjamin Franklin is the only non-twentieth century poet represented in this volume. He is included because Ross Lee Finney falls within our designated historical period and because Finney's major song cycle, Poor Richard, amply fulfills the overall parameters of this study.

2. For Ross Lee Finney's comments on his studies with Berg and Boulanger, see: Cole Gagne and Tracy Caras,

Soundpieces, Interviews with American Composers (Metuchen, N.J.: Scarecrow Press, 1982), pp. 182ff.

3. Ross Lee Finney, "Analysis and the Creative Process," Scripps College Bulletin, XXXIII: 2 (Feb. 1959), p. 10.

4. Ross Lee Finney, "Composer in Residence," Composer, XV (April 1965), pp. 5-6.

5. Ross Lee Finney, "The Composer in Academia," College Music, X (1970), pp. 76-77.

6. Ross Lee Finney, "Employ the Composer," American Music Teacher, XI: 2 (1961), p. 9.

7. Ibid.

8. Ross Lee Finney, "Theory in a Period of Change," American Music Teacher, XVII: 1 (1967), p. 45.

9. Gilbert Chase, America's Music (New York: McGraw-Hill, 1966), p. 614.

10. Ross Lee Finney, Three Seventeenth Century Lyrics (Northampton: Valley Music Press, 1938).

11. Paul Cooper, "The Music of Ross Lee Finney," The Musical Quarterly, LIII: 1 (Jan. 1967), p. 4. This article by Paul Cooper, currently on the faculty of Rice University, contains a complete listing of Finney's works including publishers, recordings, and first performances, to 1966.

12. William Billings (1746-1800), an early New England composer.

13. For a discussion of the Ainsworth Psalter and its musical descendants, see H. Wiley Hitchcock, Music in the United States (Englewood Cliffs, N.J.: Prentice-Hall, 1969), p. 4.

14. Ross Lee Finney, "Poor Richard" (New York: G. Schirmer, 1950). Tenor. Range: d^1 to a^2.

15. Carl Van Doren, Benjamin Franklin (New York: Viking, 1938), pp. 114-115.

16. Francis Hopkinson (1737-1791), the first native born

American composer. For an extensive treatment of Hopkinson, see Hitchcock, Music in the United States, p. 33.

17. Letter of September 23, 1982, to the author.

18. Hitchcock, p. 225.

19. Van Doren, p. 145.

20. W. Thomas Marrocco and Harold Gleason, Music in America (New York: W. W. Norton, 1964), p. 105.

21. Van Doren, p. 148.

22. Ibid.

23. Letter of August 17, 1982, to the author. George Newton has been serving for the past several years as interim associate editor of music reviews for the Bulletin of the National Association of Teachers of Singing.

24. Charles Naginski, "Look down, fair moon" (New York: G. Schirmer, 1942). Medium voice. Range: d^1 to e^2. Charles Naginski, "The Ship Starting" (New York: G. Schirmer, 1942). Medium voice. Range: b flat to c^2. Both of these songs are out of print. They are available from G. Schirmer as archive copies and are also held by the Library of Congress Music Division.

25. Walt Whitman, "The Last of the War Cases," November Boughs (Philadelphia: David McKay, 1888).

26. This essay, titled "Notes (such as they are) founded on Elias Hicks" is also in November Boughs.

27. Charles Naginski, "Under the harvest moon" (New York: G. Schirmer, 1940). Medium voice. Range: d^1 to e^2. Out of print. Available from G. Schirmer as an archive copy and held by the Library of Congress.

28. Louis Untermeyer, ed., Modern American Poetry (New York: Harcourt, Brace and World, 1969), p. 197.

29. Charles Naginski, "Night Song at Amalfi" (New York: G. Schirmer, 1942). Medium voice. Range: d^1 to e^2. Out of print. Held by the Library of Congress.

30. See Billy Jon Woods, "The Songs of Sergius Kagen,"

The NATS Bulletin, XXVII: 3 (1974), p. 24-5, for a complete listing of the songs. Also see Billy Jon Woods, Sergius Kagen: His Life and Works (Nashville: George Peabody College for Teachers Dissertation, 1969), for detailed biographical information and stylistic description of the songs.

31. No relation to the author, to her knowledge.

32. Sergius Kagen, "The Teaching of Carl Friedberg," The Juilliard Review, IV (Winter, 1956-57), pp. 28-32.

33. There were two daughters born of this marriage: Anna Lee (1944) and Ruth Greer (1950).

34. Sergius Kagen, "Training Accompanists at Juilliard," The Juilliard Review, VII: 1 (1959-60), p. 5.

35. Conversation of October 9, 1982, with the author.

36. Sergius Kagen, Music for the Voice (Bloomington: Indiana University Press, 1968).

37. Sergius Kagen, On Studying Singing (New York: Dover, 1960).

38. Sergius Kagen, "Mack Harrell," The Juilliard Review, VII: 2 (1960), p. 15.

39. Sergius Kagen, "The American Concert Song," The Juilliard Review, I (Fall, 1954), p. 11.

40. Ibid.

41. Ibid., p. 16.

42. Sergius Kagen, "I Think I Could Turn" (New York: Mercury Music, 1952). Bass. Range: A sharp to d^1. This song, as well as "Mag," is dedicated to Howard Swanson, himself a writer of many fine songs in the forties and fifties.

43. See Volume I of this series, p. 65, for a discussion of "Walt Whitman," an Ives setting of another portion of "Song of Myself."

44. Sergius Kagen, "Mag" (New York: Weintraub Music, 1950). Baritone. Range: B flat to e^1.

45. Sergius Kagen, "Maybe" (New York: Weintraub Music, 1950). Soprano. Range: d^1 to g^2.

46. Sergius Kagen, "A June Day" (New York: Weintraub Music, 1950). Soprano. Range: f sharp^1 to b flat^2.

47. Sergius Kagen, "Let It Be Forgotten" (New York: Weintraub Music, 1950). High voice. Range: f^1 to f^2.

48. "Quartal": harmonic system based on the fourth, as distinguished from the common system of "tertian" harmony, based on the third.

49. Interview with Paul Nordoff: Philadelphia, February 5, 1975.

50. Anthony, Silvia and Guy. In 1950, G. Schirmer published Nordoff's Anthony's Song Book which was a collection of ten play songs for children, to his own texts.

51. For a comprehensive listing of Nordoff's works, see the author's article in: Stanley Sadie, ed., The New Grove Dictionary of Music and Musicians (London: Macmillan Publishers, 1980), Volume XIII, p. 277.

52. For a clear presentation of Steiner's life and thought, see A. P. Shepherd, A Scientist of the Invisible. Publisher and date are not given in the current reprinted edition, but it is available from the Anthroposophical Press, 258 Hungry Hollow Rd., Spring Valley, N.Y.

53. See Grove's article (note 51).

54. All of this musical material has been published by Theodore Presser.

55. Nordoff described to the author (see note 49) a letter in which e.e. cummings had said "I not only like Paul Nordoff's settings, I love them." The relationship between Nordoff and cummings is also discussed in Richard S. Kennedy, Dreams in the Mirror (New York: Liveright, 1980), pp. 383-4.

56. Wife of Judge Bok and mother of Derek Bok, current president of Harvard University.

57. Conversation of July 4, 1973, with the author.

58. Quotations from this interview also appear in Volume I of this series on pages 4 and 8.

59. Frederick J. Hoffman, Conrad Aiken (New York: Twayne, 1962), preface.

60. Ibid.

61. Ibid., p. 70.

62. Stanley Kunitz and Howard Haycraft, eds., Twentieth Century Authors (New York: H. W. Wilson, 1942), p. 13.

63. See Volume I, p. 13.

64. Paul Nordoff, "White Nocturne" (Philadelphia: Oliver Ditson, 1942). Medium voice. Range: e^1 to e^2. Out of print. Held by the Library of Congress. This song is recorded in John Hanks and Ruth Friedberg, Art Song in America (Durham, N. C.: Duke University Press, 1966).

65. Neil Corcoran, "Conrad Aiken," Great Writers of the English Language--Poets (New York: St. Martin's, 1979), p. 14.

66. Untermeyer, Modern American Poetry, p. 419.

67. Paul Nordoff, "Music I heard with you" (London: Schott, 1938). High voice. Range: d sharp^1 to f sharp^2. Out of print. Held by the Library of Congress (foreign copyright deposits).

68. Untermeyer, p. 420.

69. Paul Nordoff, "This is the shape of the leaf" (London: Schott, 1938). Medium voice. Range: b to e^2. Out of print. Held by the Library of Congress (foreign copyright deposits).

70. Paul Nordoff, "Fair Annette's Song" (London: Schott, 1938). High voice. Range: e^1 to f^2. Out of print. Held by the Library of Congress (foreign copyright deposits). Notice that Nordoff changes the spelling of the title which reads "Fair Annet's Song" in Howe's setting and in the original poem. This could, of course, have been a printer's error.

BIBLIOGRAPHY

A. Bibliographical Tools

Dictionary Catalog of the Music Collection. New York Public Library.

Dissertation Abstracts International. Ann Arbor, Michigan: University Microfilms, 1938--.

Granger, Edith, ed. Index to Poetry and Recitations. Chicago: A. C. McClurg and Co., 1918 (and supplements).

Jackson, Richard. United States Music, Sources of Bibliography and Collective Bibliography. Brooklyn, New York: Institute for Studies in American Music, 1976.

Krummel, Geil, Dyen, and Root. Resources of American Music History. Urbana, Illinois: University of Illinois Press, 1981.

Mead, Rita. Doctoral Dissertations in American Music, A Classified Bibliography. Brooklyn, New York: Institute for Studies in American Music, 1974.

Music Index. Annual index to articles on music in various periodicals, 1949--.

B. American Music

Bloch, Adrienne Fried and Neuls-Bates, Carol, eds.

200

Women in American Music. Westport, Connecticut: Greenwood Press, 1979.

Chase, Gilbert. America's Music. New York: McGraw-Hill, 1966.

Finney, Ross Lee. "Analysis and the Creative Process," Scripps College Bulletin, XXXIII: 2 (Feb. 1959), pp. 1-17.

_____. "Employ the Composer," American Music Teacher, XI: 2 (1961), pp. 8-9.

_____. "Theory in a Period of Change," American Music Teacher, XV: 2 (1967), pp. 22-23.

Gagne, Cole and Caras, Tracy. Soundpieces; Interviews with American Composers. Metuchen, New Jersey: Scarecrow, 1982.

Hitchcock, H. Wiley. Music in the United States: A Historical Introduction. Englewood Cliffs, New Jersey: Prentice-Hall, 1969.

Howard, John Tasker. Our American Music. New York: Crowell, 1965.

Kagen, Sergius. "The Teaching of Carl Friedberg," Juilliard Review, IV (Winter, 1956-57), pp. 28-32.

_____. "Training Accompanists at Juilliard," Juilliard Review, VII: 1 (1959-60), p. 5.

_____. "Mack Harrell," Juilliard Review, VII: 2 (1960), p. 15.

Marrocco, W. Thomas and Gleason, Harold. Music in America. New York: W. W. Norton, 1964.

Thomson, Virgil. The Art of Judging Music. New York: Knopf, 1948.

_____. American Music Since 1910. New York: Holt, Rinehart and Winston, 1971.

C. American Art Song

Friedberg, Ruth C. "The Songs of John Duke," NATS
Bulletin, XIX: 4 (May, 1963), pp. 8-13.

_____. "Six Poems of Emily Dickinson" (review),
NATS Bulletin, XXXV: 3 (Jan./Feb., 1979), pp. 38-
39.

_____. "The Recent Songs of John Duke," NATS Bul-
letin, XXXVI: 1 (Sept./Oct., 1979), pp. 31-36.

_____. American Art Song and American Poetry,
Volume I. Metuchen, New Jersey: Scarecrow, 1981.

Kagen, Sergius. "The American Concert Song," Juilliard
Review, I (Fall, 1954), pp. 11-16.

Woods, Billy Jon. "The Songs of Sergius Kagen," NATS
Bulletin, XXVII: 3, pp. 24-5.

D. Composers

Anderson, E. Ruth, comp. Contemporary American Com-
posers. Boston: G. K. Hall, 1976.

Cooper, Paul. "The Music of Ross Lee Finney," The
Musical Quarterly, LIII: 1 (Jan., 1967), pp. 1-21.

Ewen, David. Composers Since 1900. New York: H.
W. Wilson, 1969.

Goss, Madeleine. Modern Music Makers. New York:
Dutton, 1952.

Hoover, Kathleen and Cage, John. Virgil Thomson, His
Life and Music. Freeport, New York: Books for Li-
braries Press, 1959.

Howe, Mary, obituary. Peabody Notes, XVIII: 2 (Win-
ter, 1965).

Kagen, Sergius. On Studying Singing. New York: Dov-
er, 1960.

_____. Music for the Voice. Bloomington: Indiana
University Press, 1968.

Slonimsky, Nicholas, ed. Baker's Biographical Dictionary of Musicians. New York: Schirmer Books, 1978.

Thomson, Virgil. Virgil Thomson. New York: Knopf, 1967.

Waldrop, G. W. "Winter Colonists at the MacDowell Colony," Musical Courier, CLIII (Jan. 15, 1956), p. 26.

Woods, Billy Jon. Sergius Kagen: His Life and Works. Nashville: George Peabody College for Teachers Dissertation, 1969.

E. Poets and Poetry

Aiken, Conrad. Nocturne of Remembered Spring and Other Poems. Boston: The Four Seas Company, 1917.

Allen, Gay Wilson. Walt Whitman Handbook. New York: New York University Press, 1975.

Bishop, Elizabeth. "Efforts of Affection: A Memoir of Marianne Moore," Vanity Fair, XLVI: 4 (June, 1983), pp. 44-61.

Brittin, Norman A. Edna St. Vincent Millay. New York: Twayne, 1967.

Butscher, Edward. Adelaide Crapsey. Boston: Twayne, 1979.

Colum, Mary. Life and the Dream. Garden City, New York: Doubleday, 1947.

Cox, James M., ed. Robert Frost, A Collection of Critical Essays. Englewood Cliffs, New Jersey: Prentice-Hall, 1962.

Crapsey, Adelaide. Verse. New York: Knopf, 1922.

cummings, e.e. Complete Poems. New York: Harcourt, Brace, Jovanovich, 1972.

Deutsch, Babette. Poetry in Our Time. Garden City, New York: Doubleday, 1963.

203

Dickinson, Emily. The Complete Poems. Thomas H.
Johnson, ed. Boston: Little, Brown, 1960.

Drake, William. Sara Teasdale, Woman and Poet. San
Francisco: Harper and Row, 1979.

Ellmann and O'Clair, eds. The Norton Anthology of Mod-
ern Poetry. New York: W. W. Norton, 1973.

Engel, Bernard F. Marianne Moore. New York: Twayne,
1964.

Franchere, Hoyt C. Edwin Arlington Robinson. New
York: Twayne, 1968.

Franklin, Benjamin. The Sayings of Poor Richard (col-
lected and edited by Paul Leicester Ford). New York:
The Knickerbocker Press, 1890.

Friedman, Norman. e.e. cummings, The Art of His
Poetry. Baltimore: The Johns Hopkins Press, 1960.

_____. e.e. cummings, The Growth of a Writer.
Carbondale, Illinois: Southern Illinois University
Press, 1964.

Frost, Robert. Complete Poems. New York: Holt,
Rinehart and Winston, 1962.

Funnell, Bertha H. Walt Whitman on Long Island. Port
Washington, New York: Kennikat Press, 1971.

Gerber, Philip L. Robert Frost. Boston: Twayne,
1966.

Gould, Jean. The Poet and her Book, a biography of
Edna St. Vincent Millay. New York: Dodd, Mead,
1969.

Gray, Thomas. Elinor Wylie. New York: Twayne,
1969.

Gregory, Horace and Zaturenska, Marya. A History of
American Poetry (1900-1940). New York: Harcourt,
Brace, 1942.

Hadas, Pamela White. Marianne Moore. Syracuse,
New York: Syracuse University Press, 1977.

Hoffman, Frederick J., Allen, Charles, and Ulrich, Carolyn F. The Little Magazine. Princeton: Princeton University Press, 1947.

Hoffman, Frederick J. Conrad Aiken. New York: Twayne, 1962.

Holland, Lawrence B., ed. The Norton Anthology of American Literature, Vol. 2. New York: W. W. Norton, 1979.

Kennedy, Richard S. Dreams in the Mirror (a biography of e.e. cummings). New York: Liveright, 1980.

Kunitz, Stanley and Haycraft, Howard, eds. Twentieth Century Authors. New York: H. W. Wilson, 1942.

Kunitz and Haycraft, eds. Twentieth Century Authors, First Supplement. New York: H. W. Wilson, 1961.

Lowell, Amy. The Complete Poetical Works. Boston: Houghton, Mifflin, 1955.

Mariani, Paul. William Carlos Williams. New York: McGraw-Hill, 1981.

Marks, Barry A. e.e. cummings. New York: Twayne, 1964.

Martin, Jay. Conrad Aiken, A Life of His Art. Princeton: Princeton University Press, 1962.

Merton, Thomas. The Seven Storey Mountain. New York: Harcourt, Brace, 1948.

Millay, Edna St. Vincent. Collected Poems. New York: Harper and Row, 1956.

Millett, Fred B. Contemporary American Authors, A Critical Survey. New York: AMS Press, 1970 (Reprinted from 1940 edition: Harcourt, Brace and World).

Moore, Marianne. Tell Me, Tell Me. New York: Viking, 1966.

Moritz, Charles, ed. Current Biography. New York: H. W. Wilson, 1968.

Nitchie, George W. Marianne Moore, An Introduction
to the Poetry. New York: Columbia University Press,
1969.

Norman, Charles. e.e. cummings, The Magic-Maker.
New York: Duell, Sloan and Pearce, 1964.

Olson, Stanley. Elinor Wylie, A Life Apart. New York:
Dial, 1979.

Robinson, Edwin Arlington. Collected Poems. New York:
Macmillan, 1922.

Robinson, W. R. Edwin Arlington Robinson. A Poetry
of the Act. Cleveland: The Press of Western Re-
serve University, 1967.

Sandburg, Carl. Good Morning, America. New York:
Harcourt, Brace and Co., 1928.

Sanders, G. D. and Nelson, J. H., eds. Chief Modern
Poets of England and America. New York: Macmil-
lan, 1929.

Sewall, Richard B., ed. Emily Dickinson, A Collection
of Critical Essays. Englewood Cliffs, New Jersey:
Prentice-Hall, 1963.

_____. The Lyman Letters--New Light on Emily Dick-
inson and Her Family. Amherst: The University of
Massachusetts Press, 1965.

_____. The Life of Emily Dickinson. New York:
Farrar, Straus and Giroux, 1974.

Smith, Susan Sutton, ed. The Complete Poems and Col-
lected Letters of Adelaide Crapsey. Albany, New York:
State University of New York Press, 1977.

Teasdale, Sara. Collected Poems. New York: Mac-
millan, 1966.

Untermeyer, Louis, ed. Modern American Poetry. New
York: Harcourt, Brace and World, 1969.

Van Doren, Carl. Benjamin Franklin. New York: Vik-
ing, 1938.

Van Doren, Mark. The Autobiography of Mark Van Doren. New York: Harcourt, Brace, 1958.

_____. Collected and New Poems. New York: Hill and Wang, 1963.

Vinson, James, ed. Great Writers of the English Language--Poets. New York: St. Martin's, 1979.

Waggoner, Hyatt H. American Poets from the Puritans to the Present. New York: Dell Publishing, 1968.

West, Rebecca, ed. Selected Poems of Carl Sandburg. New York: Harcourt, Brace and World, 1926.

Whitman, Walt. Complete Poetry and Selected Prose and Letters. London: Nonesuch Press, 1967.

Wylie, Elinor. Collected Poems. New York: Knopf, 1932.

F. Poetry and Song

Day-Lewis, C. The Lyric Impulse. Cambridge, Massachusetts: Harvard University Press, 1965.

Duke, John. "Some Reflections on the Art Song in English," The American Music Teacher, XXV: 4 (Feb/March, 1976), p. 26.

_____. "The Significance of Song," Ars Lyrica, I: 1 (1981), pp. 11-21.

Langer, Susanne. Philosophy in a New Key. Cambridge, Massachusetts: Harvard University Press, 1951.

_____. Feeling and Form. New York: Scribner's, 1953.

_____. Problems of Art. New York: Scribner's, 1957.

APPENDIX I: INDEX OF SONGS CITED

213

GENERAL INDEX

215

Harvard Advocate 184
Harvard Glee Club 27
Harvard Monthly 108, 184
Harvard Music Review 108
Norton Professorship of Poetry 109
Hasard, Donald 51
H.D. 22
Heine, Heinrich 14
Hemingway, Ernest 27
Hichborn, Philip 10
Hicks, Elias 160
Higginson, Thomas 129
Hill, Edward Burlingame 27, 143
Hopkinson, Francis 147, 154
Howe, Mary 3, 7-21, 23-26, 47, 76, 77, 193-194
  Baritone Songs 9
  "Chain Gang Song" 9
  English Songs: Part One 9, 20
  English Songs: Part Two 9
  English Songs: Part Three 9
  "Fair Annet's Song" 20, 193-194
  French Songs 9
  German Songs 9
  "Let Us Walk in the White Snow" 11, 14-16
  "Little Elegy" 11-14
  "Prinkin' Leddie" 20-21
  "Robin Hood's Heart" 11
  Seven Goethe Songs 9
  "Spring Pastoral" 11
  "Three Hokku" 23-26
  "When I Died in Berners Street" 11, 17-19
Howe, Walter Bruce 8
Hughes, Langston 172
Hugo, Victor 31, 34, 36
Hutcheson, Ernest 8

Illinois, University of 118
  Illinois Magazine 118
Imagism 4, 5, 22, 31, 65, 93, 172
Impressionism 5, 25
Ives, Charles 159, 162
  "The Swimmers" 162
Ivey, Donald 13

221

224